Baby Boomers' Retirement Survival Guide

How to Navigate Through the Turbulent Times Ahead

By Rich Paul

ISBN: 1479161969
ISBN-13: 978-1479161966

"There is a Chinese curse which says 'May he live in interesting times.' Like it or not, we live in interesting times."
— Robert F. Kennedy, June 6, 1966.

If only Bobby Kennedy could see us now…

Acknowledgments

My inspiration for writing *The Baby Boomers' Retirement Survival Guide* came from my growing concern that many of my fellow baby boomers may be falling substantially short of the mark when it comes to preparing themselves financially for retirement. It is my hope that this book will show readers the steps needed to ensure a successful retirement and encourage them to take those steps. Because of our country's ever-changing economic landscape, I believe that there has never been a more critical time for those of our generation to make sure that the financial pathway they are on is a prudent one that will lead to financial independence.

For all of you reading my book, I personally want to commend you for seeking to educate yourself on this complex topic. I encourage you to remain diligent in your quest for knowledge, because the decisions you make in regard to your retirement will likely be the most important decisions you will ever make.

This book would not have been possible without the tremendous support from my staff. I am truly blessed to be surrounded by such hard-working and efficient individuals. I would like to recognize Wendy Haworth, my associate advisor, and the person I refer to as "my right arm." While I was dedicating countless hours to writing this book, her dedication and commitment to overseeing the office was exceptional. In addition, she never tired or complained of reading the drafts and giving her honest opinions, some of which led me in completely different directions.

A project like this cannot be completed without an enormous amount of hours of research, so I would like to thank my two sons, Steve and Matt, for all of their assistance in compiling data and helping me to stay organized. It goes without saying that my wife, Michele, who has been constantly by my side, is a true godsend to me in so many aspects of my life, and this project is certainly no exception. Her love and support has been invaluable.

I also want to personally thank my friend and copy-editor, Tom Bowen. His patience and encouragement kept the project going. He piloted my thoughts and wisdom on this important information and was a true catalyst in the production of this book.

Most important, I want to thank my Lord and Savior, who has blessed me with the gift of being able to help people obtain financial independence, something which continues to give me immeasurable satisfaction in life. He has also surrounded me with extraordinary people in my workplace, which makes my job a true joy every day. Through Him, all things are possible and we must never forget to thank Him each day for the countless blessings He bestows on each and every one of us. I can do all things through Christ who strengthens me (Philippians 4:13)

Table of Contents

Preface

The title of this book, *"Baby Boomers' Retirement Survival Guide"* came to me one night as I was driving home from work. I was mentally replaying a conversation I had earlier in the day with a couple who had worked hard all their lives, saving carefully for two things: their children's education and their own retirement. They had never sought financial advice and had relied mainly on the suggestions of their co-workers and relatives for where to invest. Here they were, on the eve of their retirement, and the nest egg they were counting on to get them through their sunset years had just lost a considerable amount after an unexpected stock market downturn.

They had figured that, between their Social Security checks and the money from their investments, they could continue to live the lifestyle to which they had grown accustomed and even travel to some places on their someday-we-will-go-there list. With the setback they had just experienced, now they were not so sure. To make matters worse, they received conflicting advice from so many about what to do now. Some advised them to stay put. "Just hang in there," they were told. "The market always bounces back." Others advised them to buy real estate. "Land is one thing that will always increase in value" said one friend. A co-worker insisted that gold was the best way to weather any economic storm. The couple was confused and worried.

I will never forget the comment the wife made to her husband at one point in our interview. She turned to him and said, "This is so overwhelming, how are we ever going to figure out which direction we should take?" I will come back to this couple later in this book.

As I drove home that evening, it occurred to me that people become paralyzed and end up without a plan because of fear of the unknown and of doing the wrong thing. The world can be a scary place if you do not have enough money. It is sometimes a scary place even if you do! But if you don't, it can be as terrifying as being lost in the wilderness without protection from the elements and in danger from predators, or being out in a turbulent sea, whipsawed by erratic currents and without the lifesaving equipment needed for rescue or navigation.

This couple's concern was justified. I wondered how many others of their age group had similar fears about the future now that they were approaching retirement. I have read that, in the United States, a baby boomer turns sixty every eight seconds. Millions of this iconic generation—which had fearlessly faced the new frontier and learned to live with the nuclear age—are turning a new page in their lives and facing an altogether new challenge: maintaining their independence and making their money last for the rest of their lives.

Braving the Wilderness

It was the summer of 1995. My two children, Steve and Matt, ages ten and seven respectively, were typical boys, active and energetic. A free weekend was coming up, and I suggested that we all go camping. I have to confess right here and now that I am a city dweller by heritage and by choice. My idea of "roughing it" is to stay at a motel without a workout room! But I am also a good dad, and every good dad takes his kids camping at least once in his lifetime to show them what it's like to rough it for a day or two.

When I told the kids about my idea, they were excited. My wife, Michele, not so much. She knew that I had no idea how to set up our new tent. In any case, she opted out of our adventure but did agree to help us pack for the great outdoors.

In this case, the "great outdoors" turned out to be Oak Grove Park. Not knowing quite where to go, we chose a strategic spot. While not quite the wilderness area I had at first imagined, it was within walking distance of a lake with a beach. We were able to find plenty of camping spots close to restrooms with running water. Fire pits were close by, which eliminated the need to build a campfire for cooking. We were very close to a parking area, which eliminated the need for strenuous hiking. Hey, roughing it wasn't so bad.

So, while we did not forage for berries and nuts for food, and we did not build our own fire from scratch, we did sleep in a tent for the night. And we did tell ghost stories. And we created a memory we will always have. The memory of that "wilderness" experience is as fresh today as if it had happened yesterday. I remember lying there in the quiet of the tent after the boys had gone to sleep, thinking about my family and how fortunate I was to have them. I also longed for the comfort of a soft bed. So, I confess that I know nothing about survival in the wild (an information deficit I hope I am never forced to regret). But because of my training and experience, I have learned a thing or two about *financial* survival, and I hope to share some of this knowledge with you in the pages of this book.

Financial survival for retiring baby boomers in this day and age calls for knowledge and its application in a plan of action. No matter how concise and beneficial the information in any survival guide, directions not acted on are useless.

As you read this book, you may come across new avenues of thought and concepts that may be unfamiliar to you. I hope that you approach them with an open mind. Allow yourself to wander down these pathways for a distance—long enough to determine if they just might present a valid option for you in planning your financial future in retirement. Ideas have the power to change our lives. As ideas come up in these pages, please allow your imagination free rein to see whether they might fit your situation. If even one of them has a positive impact, then I will have accomplished my goal in putting this project together.

Introduction

Public speaking is on the top-ten list of things most feared. It's right up there with snakes and death. But I actually enjoy it.

Most often, the groups I speak to are either retirees or those approaching retirement, and they have come to hear me talk about the financial side of this new chapter in their lives. Typically, they are a crowd of strangers, both to me and to each other. They have come because of an advertisement that piqued their curiosity or because they received a direct invitation from my staff. But one thing has always intrigued me about audiences is they sometimes seem to have a collective personality. It is a phenomenon I cannot explain, but it is there. It is almost as if they got together before the meeting and came to a joint decision about whether they would be friendly or reserved, serious or jovial, loud or quiet, or some combination in between. There is usually no obvious causal factor. For instance, the weather does not seem to influence it. In fact, some of the most cheerful groups show up on the gloomiest of days. I have noticed, however, that current events do have some effect.

This happened a few years ago when I addressed a group just after the stock market had taken a nose dive during what's now called the Flash Crash. As the couples filtered in, I could feel their anxiety, and I could see real fear and deep concern on their faces. Some were angry, too. I later learned that some of them had had panicked and liquidated their entire portfolios to cash and experienced unnecessary losses. They felt betrayed by the system and they were confused about how such a crash could happen now. I was here to talk to them about money, and their mood seemed to say: "OK, how are you different from others in this system that just failed us?"

These investors had been financially injured. The injuries in this room were, for the most part, not fixable. They were the result of taking on too much risk with little or no protection from market downside volatility. Only time, a commodity most of these folks did not have in abundance, could help them recover their losses.

It occurred to me then that my work was more like that of a safety trainer whose job is to prevent the accident from happening in the first place. Financially speaking, I am a practitioner of preventive medicine. To continue with the medical metaphor, I am not the surgeon who cuts out the cancer and sews the patient up. I am the life coach who helps them prevent the disease in the first place. Did these people need my help? Absolutely! It would have been so much better, however, if I could have gotten to them earlier and prevented the damage.

Laughter, it has been said, is the shortest distance between two people. To get my tense audience to relax, I showed them a brief video that had no financial planning value, but was a good-natured poke at the world of investing. In this clip, a woman on the left side of the screen is on the phone to her broker, who is on the right side of the screen. Concerned about her account losing money, she asks the broker for advice. He calmly tells her that the situation is temporary and that the market will rebound. While he is talking, he is slowly making his way over to a window overlooking a cityscape below. Still smiling and talking, he opens the window and jumps. You see him coming at you, his tie fluttering, a smile on his face, still on the phone. The clip ends with him in this free-fall, telling the woman, "It's a great time to invesssssst!" The clip always gets a chuckle, but this time the laughter was loud and long. The video had obviously struck a chord of truth with these folks. Brokers do not know, because nobody knows (and you will hear this theme repeated often in this book) which way a market will go on any given day—or year, for that matter.

What follows in this book is largely preventive in nature. It is what I would have liked to have discussed with these people before the market crash. The concepts and ideas contained here can do little to affect the past, but they can prevent a dismal future. There's an old saying: "The roadblock to learning is not ignorance; it is the illusion of knowledge." In this book, I will try to separate investing fact from investing fiction and debunk investing myths that have caused so many to lose their way.

I once knew a man who would not travel by air. He would willingly ride cross country on a bus, train, or an automobile, but if the mode of transportation left the ground, he wanted no part of it. I asked him why he felt this way, and he told me what a disaster his first (and last) airplane ride had been. The flight itself was through turbulent skies, and he said that he had spent most of his time thinking he was going to die. The food served on the plane (this was when they still served hot meals on planes), was not to his liking. He said he found it difficult to enjoy a meal when he feared for his life. His fears may not stand up to statistics or logic, but they are intensely real to him. Feelings, after all, seem to be facts.

What about us? We often make decisions based not on facts, but on the feelings we accumulate through our experiences. Perhaps you have had a disappointing experience with stocks, and now you want nothing to do with the stock market. Perhaps you owned corporate bonds, and the corporation declared bankruptcy. Now you want nothing to do with bonds. Maybe your real estate trust stopped paying dividends, or maybe reduced them by half. Now you have a sour taste for that asset class. Perhaps your aunt had an annuity, and it was the wrong kind for her. You do not know annuities, but you do know your aunt, and you are now ready to cross annuities off the list.

All I ask is that you check your opinions at the door as you read what you find here, and let the facts influence your thinking. I believe that, in the end, you will be amazed at what you thought you knew—but didn't really know.

PART ONE

Defining Retirement in the Twenty-First Century

CHAPTER ONE

So, What is a Baby Boomer, Anyway?

"Today there are about 40 million retirees receiving benefits; by the time all the baby boomers have retired, there will be more than 72 million retirees drawing Social Security benefits."
—Tony Snow

Journalist Tom Brokaw coined the term (and titled a book) *The Greatest Generation* to describe the generation that grew up in the United States during the Great Depression and experienced World War II. Baby boomers are, for the most part, the children of the greatest generation. Baby boomers are those born from 1946 through 1964, a time marked by an unprecedented jump in birthrates across the country. Those babies are now turning sixty-five, and looking at retirement, which is why we need to talk.

Brokaw wrote another generational book about the baby boomers entitled *Boom*, where he says of this group:

> *Boom! One minute it was Ike and the man in the gray flannel suit, and the next minute it was time to 'turn on, tune in, and drop out.' While Americans were walking on the moon, Americans were dying in Vietnam. Jackie Kennedy*

became Jackie O. There were tie-dye shirts and hard hats, Black Power and law and order, Martin Luther King, Jr. and George Wallace, Ronald Reagan and Tom Hayden, Gloria Steinem and Anita Bryant, Mick Jagger and Wayne Newton. Well, you get the idea.

Simply by the sheer force of their numbers, members of this generation are a demographic bulge that has been likened to a "pig in a python." As they have passed through society, they have altered it dramatically as no other generation has done before.

In his white paper, "The Economic Impact of Aging U.S. Baby Boomers," Phillip Longman points out that baby boomers earned more at every stage of life than any other generation in history; however, they are ill prepared for retirement due to the fact they weren't the best savers.[1]

Why was that? For one reason, there were just so many toys that came along after World War II that boomers just found them hard to resist. The capitalist world was awash with luxury automobiles, color televisions, high-fidelity stereos, and gadgets of every description. Consumer credit came of age, and plastic could buy whatever the cash could not. This generation, unlike the one before it, had no recollection of hard times and bread lines. The world was their oyster and pearls were expected!

Along with the apparent prosperity of the baby boomers came more taxes. Uniquely relevant to the economic landscape of this

---

[1] Longman, Phillip. "The Economic Impact of Aging US Baby Boomers." NewAmerica.net. July 5, 2008. http://newamerica.net/files/Longman-Remarks.pdf.

generation, especially the vast working-class majority, was the payroll tax, or Social Security and Medicare tax (FICA), as we call it today. The payroll tax of the generation before was only two or three percent. By the time the first Baby Boomers took on part-time summer jobs, the payroll tax had already doubled to 7.25%. Today it is double that! According to Tom Curry, national affairs writer for MSNBC, in 1960, the beginning wage earner paid approximately $70 per year in payroll taxes. Only the first $4,800 of income was taxed, and at the modest rate of only 3%. The amount subject to taxation now is above $100,000 and climbing each year.

Payroll Tax Rate History

SOCIAL SECURITY TAX RATE		
Year	Employee and Employer Combined	Self-Employed
1940	2%	Not applicable
1950	3%	Not applicable
1960	6%	4.5%
1970	8.4%	6.3%
1980	10.16%	7.05%
1990	12.4%	12.4%
2000	12.4%	12.4%
2010	12.4%	12.4%

One reason the payroll tax burden is so much heavier today is that fifty years ago, there was no Medicare. That came along with President Lyndon B. Johnson's "Great Society" domestic programs in 1965, right around the time the earliest of the baby boomers were finishing high school and were either entering college, fighting the Vietnam War, or hoping to avoid it. Workers in 1960 didn't have to pay the 1.45% Medicare tax that workers pay today. The Medicare tax applies to all earned income, not just the first $100,000 and change, as the Social Security tax does.

As the baby boom generation ages, an interesting thing is happening with the Social Security system that eventually affects all of us. The number of people receiving money from the system increases while the number of people paying into it decreases. It's not hard to see where that's headed.

CHAPTER TWO

Challenges Lie Ahead for Most Boomers

"Today, Medicare provides health insurance to about 40 million seniors and disabled individuals each year. The number is only expected to grow as the baby boomers begin retiring."

—Jim Bunning

As of this writing, Wall Street remains volatile. Many retirees, and soon-to-be retirees, have seen as much as 30% of their retirement accounts disappear within the past few years. The economy remains unstable, without any *sustained* recovery in sight, at least not any time soon.

Our nation recently hit its "debt ceiling," racking up more than $16 trillion in unpaid bills. What is the debt ceiling exactly? It's a cap set by Congress on the amount of debt the federal government can legally borrow. The cap applies to debt owed to the public (that is, anyone who buys US bonds), plus debt owed to federal government trust funds, such as Social Security and Medicare. It makes a good case for people who worry that the future of those government-backed programs appears more uncertain than ever before.

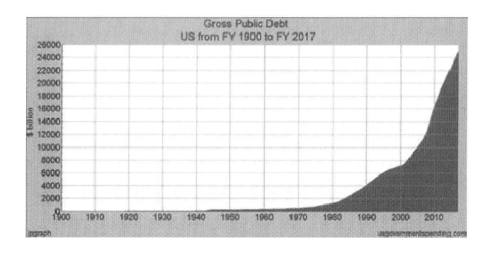

The baby boom generation faces different times and different struggles than those faced by our parents. When our parents and grandparents retired, they likely had some personal savings, and they could count on the certainty of Social Security as a second leg of income in retirement. Many had pensions from their employer. These pensions guaranteed them a lifetime income. Today, with pensions having become an endangered species and Social Security on the ropes, what's left for this generation of retirees is the burden of managing their own retirement savings in such a way that it will last for the rest of their lives. Susan Jacoby, in an article that appeared recently in the *Los Angeles Times*, gave an overview of what she called the "nest egg myth."[2] According to her, boomers are reaching retirement age but many aren't sufficiently well-off to stop working, and even those who are wealthy enough to have some sort of nest egg have far too little in it. The

2   Jacoby, Susan. "The Nest-Egg Myth." Los Angeles Times. February 20, 2011. http://articles.latimes.com/2011/feb/20/opinion/la-oe-jacoby-aging-boomers-20110220.

statistics she puts forth, obtained from Federal Reserve data analyzed by the *Wall Street Journal* and Boston College's Center for Retirement Research, are revealing and somewhat startling:

- About 50%—the amount of wealth lost by baby boomer households between 2004 and 2009, due to shrinking 401(k) accounts and the real estate collapse.
- Only 50%—the share of working Americans that have tax-sheltered retirement accounts.
- About 75%—the number of Americans over sixty-five whose annual income (including Social Security) is less than $34,000, according to a report from the Congressional Research Service. "Furthermore, household income drops precipitously with every decade, and most of the poor in their eighties and nineties are women, who—unless their husbands possessed vast wealth—are very likely to become poorer when they are widowed."
- Around 85%—the assumed share of a household's pre-retirement income needed to maintain the same standard of living in retirement.
- $87,700—the median income, in 2009, for households nearing retirements (aged sixty to sixty-two) that have 401(k)-type accounts.
- $74,545—85% of that salary is needed to retain a pre-retirement standard of living.
- As much as $35,080 a year—the amount Social Security will provide for such a household.

- $36,465—the amount needed from other sources to maintain pre-retirement standard of living. "Most 401(k) accounts don't come close to making up that gap," says E. S. Browning in the *Wall Street Journal*[3].
- $149,400—the amount the median 401(k) plan holds, according to the Center for Retirement Research.
- $9,073—amount per year such an account would provide a household, less than 25% of the $36,465 needed.
- Around 9%—the current median amount that people contribute to 401(k) plans, including employer contributions, according to Vanguard Group, a leading provider of the plans. "In general, people facing problems today got too little advice, or bad advice," says Browning. "They didn't realize that a 6% annual contribution, with a 3% company match, might not be enough."
- Between 12% and 15%—amount, including employer contribution, that Vanguard recommends people contribute to their 401(k) plan. (Sources: *Los Angeles Times*, *Wall Street Journal*)

The statistics aren't pretty, but baby boomers need to know what they're up against. Because of recent economic developments in America, the topic of conversation among many older Americans who are just now getting accustomed to being called "seniors," is not "Where will I travel when I retire?" but

---

3 Browning, E.S. "Retiring Boomers Find 401(k) Plans Fall Short." Wall Street Journal, 19 Feb. 2011. <http://online.wsj.com/article/SB10001424 052748703959604576152792748707356.html>.

"What kind of part-time work can I find in retirement?" With the advent of what's being called the Great Recession of 2008, more and more Americans are finding it necessary to put off retirement until they reach the age of seventy or beyond simply because they need the paychecks. They need the time to build their savings and they need their paychecks to make ends meet.

As a baby boomer, I never thought the boom would be the sound of my retirement account collapsing.

Unemployed Older Americans

According to Susan M. Sipprelle, columnist for the multimedia documentary project, "Over 50 and Out of Work," *unemployment* in the community of older Americans is now a problem[4].

---

4 Eisenberg, Richard. "Set For Life: A Must-See Film on Being Over 50 and Out of Work." Forbes Magazine, 30 Oct. 2012. <http://www.forbes.com/sites/nextavenue/2012/10/30/set-for-life-a-must-see-film-on-being-over-50-and-out-of-work/>.

She points out that there are millions of seniors who want to work but have been laid off and can't find jobs or have seen their businesses fail and are having difficulty getting a fresh start. Those who are looking for work face protracted job searches, and many, having given up on finding jobs, are forced to claim Social Security benefits earlier than they had intended. Others take whatever jobs they can get and settle for low wages.

Adding to this woeful state is the fact that many unemployed older Americans have found it necessary to dip into their retirement savings to make ends meet, shrinking the size of their nest egg even more. In interviews conducted with these unemployed older Americans, Sipprelle found that many of these individuals, even after reeducating themselves, spent more than a year on the job-hunting trail before landing a position. They have started over but are now deeper in debt and with dim hopes of retiring comfortably.

A Time for Caution

As with any resource, conservation of money is critically important when there may be a shortage. People who live in areas of the United States where hurricanes occur frequently have a choice to make as it become clear that they are in the storm's path. They will either opt to evacuate or hunker down and ride it out. Most of those who choose the latter know that the first thing they should do in preparation for the hurricane is to collect water. It is at the top of the checklist of things to do. The instructions say: "Fill the bathtub with water for sanitary reasons and collect as much water as you can in plastic containers for cooking and drinking purposes." Storm surges tend to compromise the safety of the water supply in low lying areas. And if the power is knocked out, you will not only use the water in the tub to wash with, but you will need it to flush the toilets. Even if water pressure is supplied by gravity from water towers, if the electrical pumps can't work and there is no generator backup system, no water will flow.

If we know there is a possibility of a money shortage in our older years, then more than ever it makes sense to conserve what we have while accumulating as much as possible without risk. When you were younger, you were able to accept more risk. You had time on your side. You could take a market downturn in stride. Markets rebound. They always have. But when we enter the "retirement red-zone," we have to think differently because our time horizon has changed.

A significant number of the people I work with on income planning are either a few short years away from retirement, or are folks who have just retired. In my interviews with them I always ask them to rate their risk tolerance on a scale of one to ten—one being the least tolerant, and ten being the most tolerant of risk.

"Put me down for a *ten*," said one man, "No pain, no gain!" he continued. He had just retired and his wife, who was seated beside him, was three years behind him. She shot him a glance that reminded me of that old expression: "If looks could kill."

"Put me down for *minus seven* and give us both a *three!*" she said quickly. We all had a good laugh out of the good-natured banter. But it occurred to me afterwards that many people approach very serious decisions with just that sort of naiveté when it comes to retirement. The truth is that many do not imagine that they can, through careful planning, have an adequate income in their sunset years without placing themselves in investment jeopardy. This is, in part, a result of having been influenced by perhaps well-meaning counselors who simply are not acquainted with strategies that are available today. Years ago, we may have been limited to just a few programs that would accomplish both safety and growth at the same time, but not anymore. Portfolio management techniques are now available that will allow for safety and growth at the same time. We simply have to know what they are and know how to implement them.

My retirement plan? On my sixty-fifth birthday, I'm going to lie down in a crop circle and wait to be abducted by aliens from outer space.

CHAPTER THREE

Fixing Social Security

"Our country also hungers for leadership to ensure the long-term survival of our Social Security system. With 70 million baby boomers in this country on the verge of retirement, we need to take action to shore up the system."

—Kay Bailey Hutchison

It is 1982, and it is apparent that Social Security is broke. There is enough money left for only a few more months. President Ronald Reagan and the leaders of the House and Senate appoint a fifteen-member National Committee on Social Security Reform. Led by Alan Greenspan, the committee meets to figure out what to do. They meet in, of all places, a Ramada Inn in Alexandria, Virginia, but they are not the only ones there. Protesters and lobbying groups show up, too. AARP has rented suites of rooms and the AFL-CIO has boots on the ground. Senior activist Maggie Kuhn and her Gray Panthers show up in force. The TV cameras catch it all on tape, including the chants from fifty or so demonstrators outside: "No ifs, ands, or buts— No Social Security cuts!" The rhymes are in vain, however, because there would be cuts and there would be higher taxes.

If you are a baby boomer, you are still being deeply affected by what that committee came up with, and you were not even represented there. The earliest of your bunch were still in their thirties, starting families, working hard, oblivious to how what was decided at that table would affect you. The Social Security Amendments of 1983 would, for the first time since the days of Franklin D. Roosevelt, impose a tax on Social Security benefits. The new law provided that, beginning in 1984, if your base annual income was $25,000 as a single taxpayer, or $32,000 for a married couple filing jointly, then up to 50% of your Social Security income would be treated as taxable income. The 1993 budget deal under President William Jefferson Clinton raised taxation to 85% of benefits for single beneficiaries with incomes over $34,000 and couples over $44,000.

There is a myth out there that says that in 1935, when FDR signed Social Security into law, he was asked if he would ever tax Social Security benefits. He is said to have pounded his fist on his desk and uttered what has been referred to as the Golden Promise: "I will never tax Social Security!" According to the Social Security Administration Office of Public Inquiries, Roosevelt never actually uttered those words or the even the substance of them. They point out that while Social Security benefits were not originally considered taxable income, and it was never really a *provision of the law* that they not be taxed.

The taxes on Social Security benefits hinge on how much *reportable* income you earn each year. What's included? Just about everything: Income from pensions, investments, CDs, even income from tax-free municipal bonds. If your modified adjusted gross income, plus one-half of your combined Social Security benefits, plus any tax-exempt interest you receive—called your combined income—exceeds the limits in the explanation above, then you will be taxed accordingly. Keep in mind that these threshold amounts were set in 1983 and 1993. Since then, Social Security benefits and general income have increased while these thresholds have remained constant. So they are likely to either remain in place or be raised. It is doubtful that they will be reduced or eliminated.

As it stands now, the only way to minimize this tax is to (a) reduce your income or (b) place assets in tax-deferred accounts where the interest received on them is not *reportable* (not considered to be part of your income by the IRS). Typically, gains paid on annuity balances are tax-deferred and are not reported as income on form 1040, while interest earned on CDs and gains from mutual funds are taxed. That does not mean you will never pay taxes on annuity gains. Tax deferred means just what it says. You will not pay taxes on the money from an annuity until you withdraw it. Consult your tax professional to determine whether it makes sense to move a portion of the money you currently have in CDs or equities over to an account where the taxes on the gains are deferred. In fact, it is always wise to consult with your tax professional before making any decisions in this regard, because the issue of taxation becomes more complex when you are coordinating Social Security with other sources of income.

Social Security Reform

According to Social Security trustees, the system is projected to run out of money by 2033. Many reform measures have been suggested, including raising the retirement age, raising payroll taxes, and revising the benefit formula in a number of different ways. These reforms should be phased in over several years, and most of you probably will not feel the adjustments. Real uncertainty lingers, however, as long as we can pick up a newspaper, or turn on the television, to discover that what we thought were guarantees are contingent upon what Congress decides.

The chart printed here, which can be found in the voluminous 2011 Social Security Trustees Report,[5] spells it out pretty clearly that, given the current track we are on, unless reforms are enacted, there will not be enough to go around for the next generation of Americans.

Chart D—OASI, DI, and HI Trust Fund Ratios
Old Age and Survivors Insurance, Disability Insurance, and Hospital Insurance (Assets as a percentage of annual cost)

The key dates regarding cash flows are shown in the following table.[a] Dates indicate the first year that a condition is projected to occur and to persist annually thereafter through 2085. (source 2011 Social Security Trustees Annual Report)

KEY DATES FOR THE TRUST FUNDS				
	OASI	DI	OASDI	HI
First-year outgo exceeds income excluding interest[a]	2010	2005	2010	2008
First-year outgo exceeds income including interest[a]	2023	2009	2021	2008
Year trust funds are exhausted	2035	2016	2033	2024

---

5 Blahous III, Charles P., and Robert D. Reischauer. "A Summary of the 2012 Annual Reports." Trustees Report Summary. US Social Security Administration. 2012. http://www.ssa.gov/OACT/TRSUM/index.html.

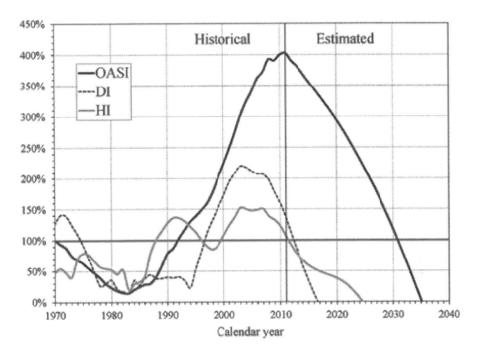

It is difficult to reach a definite conclusion about how Social Security will look for your children when they retire, or even if it will be here in its present form. Some angst publicly over this while the vast majority just pay their taxes and hope for the best. Former Vice President Al Gore popularized the term "lock box." The Social Security system is officially called a "trust" in all the documentation produced by the government, but the money that funds it seems to be left on the table for use by raiding politicians to fund government programs of many sorts. Many see their money as being misspent and far from being locked in a box for them.

If you are a baby boomer, and have not made individual plans for retirement, start now and work as long as you can. You must now play catch up. Chunk your money away as safely as possible, but keep it working for you. Get some coaching on programs that will allow you to grow your money while keeping a portion of it safe from market risk.

There are always two sides to every coin. On the one hand, if the tax on Social Security benefits had not been imposed in the 1980s and 1990s, baby boomers today would probably not be getting a monthly check at all. On the other hand, what would have happened if, at that meeting in 1983, it had been mandated that, instead of pumping more tax dollars into the government's forced retirement system, this burgeoning horde of baby boomers were allowed to pump the same amount of money into a private sector program? Some who have crunched the numbers say that the average nest egg of those now entering retirement would be nearly a half million dollars.

CHAPTER FOUR

Are 401(k)s the New Pensions for Boomers?

"The boomers' biggest impact will be on eliminating the term 'retirement' and inventing a new stage of life... the new career arc."

– Rosabeth Moss Kanter

If you have noticed the lines getting longer at the grocery store checkout counter and more cars in front of you at stoplights lately, there's a good reason for it. The population of the United States at last count was over 312 million, and we are living longer, too. In 1900, the average life expectancy was forty-seven. In 1920, it was fifty-four. By 1940, it was sixty-two, and in 2004, it was just shy of eighty. At this writing, the average projected life span is eighty-four. The National Vital Statistics System says that we are taking better care of ourselves and medical science just keeps advancing.

As I was doing research for this book, news was surfacing that scientists are in the process of successfully growing a pig's heart and that they may be five to ten

> "Children born today have a fifty-fifty chance of living to 100."
>
> *- William Greider*

years away from growing a human heart. The current thinking on longevity is that kids born today stand a reasonable chance of living past the century mark if they take care of themselves.

Here's a good news/bad news joke for you. So the lawyer says to his client: "I got good news and I got bad news. The bad news is they found your blood at the crime scene."

"What's the good news?" asks the client.

"The good news is your cholesterol is down to 103!"

The good news for baby boomers is that they are living longer. The bad news is that they are living longer.

How could living longer possibly have a downside? That's what I said. But in a new poll of people ages forty-four to seventy-five, more than three in five (61%) said they fear depleting their assets more than they fear dying. The poll, conducted by Allianz Life Insurance Company of North America, sampled opinions from 3,257 people and discovered that 92% felt that the United States is facing *a crisis in its retirement system.*[6] Now why would that be? The poll revealed that 56% feared not being able to meet their basic living expenses in retirement. Those with traditional pensions felt "calm and secure" about their retirement future, whereas those relying on 401(k) plans that track the performance of the stock market were not so confident. Keep in mind, this survey was conducted *after* the 2008 stock market correction.

The Disappearing Pension

It appears that traditional pension plans are rapidly going the way of the dinosaurs. Defined-benefit pension plans are, as their

---

6 AllianzLife. "Reclaiming the Future." white paper, 2011.

name implies, programs that "define" or clearly outline what benefits the recipients will get in retirement. Typically, they guarantee a paycheck for the rest of the retiree's life and perhaps that of the spouse, if that option is elected. The payoff is not determined by how much you contribute to the plan, or how well the stock market performs, or how well you invest. With a defined benefit pension plan, it is up to the *employer* to make sure the *employee* gets the money. The federal government is there for a backup in case the company fails. Not a bad deal, huh? So what's killing pension programs?

Once upon a time, employers valued a long-term, experienced employee, and rewarded them with a lifetime pension at the end of a career. Those days seem gone for good. The philosophy today among employers and workers is "get what you can for a few years and move on." Loyalty and long-term rewards seem to be a thing of the past for both parties. Here are a few factors that account for the pension's demise:

- Losses in the stock market. When market downturns caused losses within the plans, many companies had to make big payments to their pension funds for the first time in years. They did not like that.
- Changes in the basic structure of the US economy. Large manufacturing companies used to do everything in-house. Now it seems they outsource as much as possible. These smaller service companies to which the work is being outsourced are not large enough to sustain employee pensions like the giant companies they feed. If these smaller

companies have retirement programs at all, they are likely to be defined *contribution* plans, or 401(k) type plans.

- High turnover. Pensions reward workers who stay with one company for a long time. High turnover and shrinking job tenure has caused portable plans like 401(k)s to become more popular.
- Echelon shift. It used to be that pension plans covered management as well as workers downline; everyone from the CEO to the cleaning person participated in the same plan. Starting in the 1970s, retirement money for management began to be managed separately, reducing the incentive to keep pensions going.
- Misuse. Companies began misusing pension fund monies by "robbing Peter to pay Paul," or misappropriating plan money to meet other obligations.

Defined benefit pension horror stories are surfacing more and more frequently. The *Wall Street Journal* reported on one man's rude awakening when he retired from a major communications network where he had—or thought he had—one of the best retirement benefit packages in corporate America. But instead of traveling and enjoying the carefree life he thought he would lead in retirement, he had to get a job as a security guard to make ends meet.

What happened? His company had started tapping into the pension fund to keep its promises to newer employees. His retirement fund had been used to pay for, among other things, rising health-care premiums. Up until the 1990s, there had actually been a surplus in the plan, but stock market reversals eroded it to the point that by the time he retired, the plan was out of money and could not pay.

How to Check On Your Pension

If you have a defined benefit pension plan and you want to know if there's been any monkey business going on with it, where do you look? The one document that spells everything out is the company's annual report. The larger the company, the better the chance you have of getting all your questions answered. Companies whose stock is publicly held are obligated to publish annual reports and make them available. If you don't want to go leafing through up to two hundred pages of fine print, just go to the Internet and search for the name of the company and "annual report." It should take you right to it. Then, assuming it is a PDF document, you can use the search feature to isolate the portion of the report that discusses the pension plan. Pay particular attention to how much money the pension plan has in it, and whether it is making or losing money, and what kind of activity, if any, has gone on within the plan.

401(k) Plans Take Over

At the end of 1985, eighty-nine of the Fortune 100 companies offered traditional defined *benefit* pension plans to their employees. By 2010, only seventeen companies on the Fortune 100 list did so, and defined *contribution* plans (think 401(k)) were replacing them (data from Towers Watson Consulting).

The ascendency of the 401(k) was an exciting addition to the retirement landscape, especially during the heady days of the

1990s when all was rosy with the market. This was particularly true if the plan was accompanied by a generous company match. Unlike the old style DB pensions, 401(k)s allowed plan participants to decide how their money was to be invested. In some cases, this was not for the best. Employees who lacked knowledge about investing now had to look over their menu of choices and make serious investment decisions. They may have had some guidance from the firm the company selected to administrate the plan, but largely they were on their own. The wrong choice could cost them thousands, as some would later find out.

If the employees and the 401(k) were having a honeymoon, it probably ended with the decade of the 1990s and the bursting of Wall Street's tech bubble. As the new century dawned, many companies whose matching funds were generous before, now began to cut back. The 401(k) lost a bit more of its luster in the 2008 market correction. In more certain economic times, employees used to open the envelopes containing their 401(k) plan statements, confident of a higher balance. Now they were more likely to cringe, hoping they would not see those ugly parentheses around the numbers, signifying another loss.

No Rainbow, No Pot of Gold

Rainbows are created when raindrops reflect sunlight and break the light into different colored wavelengths. This colorful phenomenon usually occurs during a sudden summer shower while the sun is out. No one knows for sure what inspired the notion that there is a pot of gold at the end of each rainbow. Somehow the myth has come to be associated with the Irish. The legend apparently dates back to Old Europe, and it was merely enthusiastically adopted by the Irish, who first told the story that fairies put the gold there, and that leprechauns guard it. Regardless, the symbolism is obvious. The rainbow is an optical illusion, the end of which cannot be found because it isn't there. And even if you could find the end of the rainbow, I have it on good authority that there is no pot of gold there.

Baby boomers in America have come to expect that when their working days are through, there will be something like a pot of gold waiting for them. Whether through an employer's pension, or 401(k), or government plan, like Social Security and Medicare, it is taken for granted that some baseline income and healthcare benefit is out there and waiting for them. This mentality has developed mainly in the more developed countries. It is one of the things that separate the "rich" world of Europe, North America, and Japan from Third World nations, where entitlements are rare. It appears that we, as a nation, have tended to plan our saving and investing accordingly, putting away less than we would have if our retirement had to be fully self-funded.

With pensions dying out, 401(k)s susceptible to loss, and the Social Security system having to be rescued from the edge of bankruptcy, it may be time for us to remove our rose-colored glasses and see how things truly are. If there is to be a pot of gold, it will be one of our own making and filled by our efforts at earning, saving, and prudent investing, not by any rainbow pixie dust or leprechaun generosity.

CHAPTER FIVE

The Myths of Investing

"Well, the big elephant in the whole system is the baby boomer generation that marches through like a herd of elephants. And we begin to retire in 2008."
– Lindsey Graham

As we shift into a very pertinent discussion having to do with equity markets (stocks and bonds) in these next few chapters, you may be thinking: "What does this have to do with economic survival?" It has quite a lot to do with it, actually. If you get this part wrong, you could seriously endanger your retirement and potentially run out of money just when you need it the most, an outcome that must be avoided if humanly possible. To navigate through this minefield, there are several issues we need to consider, beginning with the question: "How much exposure should I have at any given time to equities?" The answer to this will be predicated on a number of different factors:

- Your risk tolerance
- Time horizon/longevity
- Your current income needs
- Your future income needs

- Your lifestyle goals
- Inflation concerns
- Liquidity concerns

For the simple reason that your retirement could extend out thirty-plus years, you're probably going to experience a doubling, if not a tripling in your cost of living. Equities have proven to be the prominent inflation fighter over other asset classes. Allocating some portion, depending on the variables above, will guide us to the correct amount that you'll need in your portfolio.

Myths are like crabgrass. They spread quickly and are difficult to get rid of. Despite the fact that we have never seen a pigeon explode at a wedding, there are still some people that believe that throwing rice after the ceremony will cause such a phenomenon.

There are even myths about the myths. One enduring myth that many baby boomers grew up with is the idea that Christopher Columbus was the only one of his time to believe the earth was round. Here is an excerpt from a textbook used in the fifties:

"When Columbus lived, people thought that the earth was flat. They believed the Atlantic Ocean to be filled with monsters large enough to devour their ship, and with fearful waterfalls over which their frail vessels would plunge to destruction. Columbus had to fight these foolish beliefs in order to get men to sail with him. He felt sure the earth was round."

It is a nice story. It's just not true. Most people of Christopher Columbus's day believed the earth to be round. They could see the round moon, and they could see that the sun was round, or at least disc shaped. Those with education had access to the wisdom of people like Aristotle, who first came up with observational evidence of a round earth.

Myths about investing are just as persistent and much more expensive for those who believe in them. Let's explore four insidious myths that cost American investors billions every year.

Myth #1
Stock Selection

This myth involves choosing stocks based on the belief that they will do well in the future, and putting one's faith in investment advisors or mutual fund managers who claim that they can consistently and predictably add value to our investment accounts by exercising some "superior skill" that they possess in selecting individual stocks.

There is a belief out there that some investment advisors just have a special knack. Maybe they were born with it. Or maybe it is just a superior skill that they have acquired. This gift, they tell you, will enable them to *consistently* and predictably pick the right stocks, and that these stocks will produce above average returns. The pitch may go something like this: "We know which stocks you should own. Just trust our analysis and our brokers and our advanced research."

Perhaps you have seen magazines proclaiming that message on their front covers. While passing through an airport terminal not too long ago, I stopped to browse the shelves of a newsstand for a magazine to read on a plane. The cover of one well-known and well-read magazine caught my eye. The unmistakable bespectacled visage of Bill Gates of Microsoft fame peered above a headline which read: *"FOUND—The Next Microsoft. The Ultimate Quest Leads to a Small, Little-Known Stock."* Lucky me! For the price of one magazine, I can be rich. All I have to do is sell everything and buy up all the shares I can in whatever stock they are talking about, and just sit back and wait for fortune to become mine.

Next to that magazine was another cover that read: *"Where to Invest—12 Breakout Stocks to Buy Now."* It would be laughable if it were not for the fact that some poor investor is likely to buy the magazine and be influenced by it. The truth is, headlines like that are designed to sell magazines. Magazines are published to solicit advertisements. The advertisers are those claiming to be able to pick stocks and time the market. The unholy alliance between the publishers and the advertisers is what drives the myth-making machine, and the ones penalized by it are those who fall for the hype.

The truth is, nobody knows which stock is going to be the next Google or Microsoft. If I knew, I would certainly use this book as an opportunity to tell you. But I don't know. And neither do the people who pretend they do. There is no guru with a gift. There is no team of trained professionals that have developed a system of reading charts and graphs so well that they can determine which stock will emerge and dominate the market. There are no algorithms that can do it either. The earth is round, and rice does not cause pigeons to explode, folks. That's all there is to it.

"We know stocks will rally, but
we don't know which ones and when."

Myth #2
Track Record Investing

This myth would have you believe that if a fund manager or a stock picker did well in the past, he or she will do well in the future. This myth recommends using past performance to determine the best investments for the future. Let's do the math on this myth.

In order to illustrate the fallacy of this assumption, let's say you are an investor, and you want to put your money in the best mutual fund out there. You're most likely to make your decision on the performance of that fund. You look for the "track record" of that fund. In your search for a superior fund manager, do you want a novice or a veteran? Obviously you want a veteran. How else will you be able to establish a track record? The longer the track record, the better, right? Ten years or better, if you can find it, right?

While Aristotle came up with the theory based on observation that the earth was round, it was actually a German scientist by the name of Copernicus (1473-1543) who proved it scientifically by experiment and data examination. So let's do some "Copernicus" on the myth of "The Investment Guru." We took the entire Morningstar (a company that rates mutual funds) database and looked at active mutual fund managers and analyzed their rates of success in beating the returns of the S&P 500 (Standard & Poor's list of 500 largest US companies) which, by the way, is the benchmark of success for mutual fund managers. On the left side of the page, we listed the percentage of mutual fund managers who were active in the years that we sampled. Across the bottom of the page, we listed the years in our sample when they were able to beat the S&P 500.

What jumped right out at us right away was that 12% of these managers never beat the S&P. They were zero for ten. Then we noticed that none of them beat the S&P every single year. The rest, of course, fell into the middle. I'm going to go out on a limb here and declare that if we just had someone throwing darts or flipping coins, we would do just as well.

Granted, there are a few out there who occasionally throw the dart at the right balloon and get it right. And when they do, you hear about it. But the media graveyard is full of gurus who got it right once or twice and made a big splash, never to be heard from again once the great wheel of chance turned against them.

Their luck ran out, and they quickly became yesterday's news. One example is Barton Biggs. Remember him? He was the one who called the technology bubble a year before it burst. He was hailed as a Wall Street prophet. When he spoke, people got out their notepads and tape recorders…for a while. But the shine was off the penny when he totally missed the true nature of the economy's problems leading up to the 2008 market crash. In fact, he predicted a boom in that year, which as we all know now, never happened. He has not made any magazine covers lately.

The fact that there are three times as many mutual funds out there than there are individual stocks should tell you something. If there truly was one guru who was the best mutual fund manager alive, how many mutual funds would we need? ONE! And how many stocks would be in it? One! And what would we call it, "The Really Big Good Fund?"

When you look at the entire universe of mutual funds in the United States over a twenty-year period of time, some fascinating facts emerge. If we were to list the top thirty funds from 1990 to 1999 we would find that they beat the S&P by double digits. So, if you are looking at this list in the year 2000 you think, "Hey these guys have it figured out!"

Here's what you may not know. Commission-based brokers are trained to use the track record of a mutual fund to sell it. The pitch may go like this: "Mr. Jones, you have three mutual funds here, and I notice that two of them are underperforming, compared to this four-star mutual fund, which has a five-year track record of beating the market by a substantial margin. What do you think we should do?"

And, of course, the obvious answer is "Let's go with *that* fund!" Bingo! It's payday for the broker. But isn't that all right with you and me if we get a better deal? That's the point. You do not necessarily get a better deal. Our list of funds that beat the S&P during the 1990s *failed* to beat the S&P in the decade which followed. Only two of the top thirty funds in the first ten years are included in the top one thousand mutual funds of the subsequent decade.

What happens to a mutual fund that underperforms? Most of the time they are quietly phased out and merged with funds that did better. What happens to the data on those phased-out funds? It is lost in the shuffle. It is whisked into the dustbin of history and forgotten. It is not even averaged in when the past performance of mutual funds is calculated. We wondered, "What would happen to the average numbers if we looked at *all* the data—for "live" funds and "dead" funds?"

Using a database provided by the Center for Research in Securities Prices at the University of Chicago, we looked at just one year, 2010, as an example. What we found was quite revealing. There were 27,542 funds open. That is more than three times as many funds as there are stocks in the US market.

Here's the astonishing truth about what's happening behind the scenes. Between 1923 and 2010, there were 46,476 funds "born." If there were about 27,000 funds open at the end of 2010 and over 46,000 born, how many had to have been killed off? *Over* 18,000! What happened to the funds that did not make it? Why do you suppose the mutual fund industry killed them off?

One alarming statistic that surfaced in this study was that the average return of the worst 200 mutual funds that were closed was ….. So it is no wonder, then, that this data is allowed to slip quietly out of the statistics.

The Worst 200 Dead Mutual Funds

-77.7%

So please repeat after me: *"Past performance is no guarantee of future success."* That disclaimer appears on the bottom of all advertisements and somewhere on each page of the prospectus. Although it is scarcely noticed and seldom discussed, that phrase means just what it says: A manager's ability to pick stocks in the past has ZERO correlation with his/her ability to do so in the future.

	1990–1999	2000–2009
All Funds Average Return	14.89	2.11
Top 30 Funds Average Return	27.15	-4.43
S&P 500 Index	18.89	1.21
CRSP 1-10 Index	18.87	1.95
Total # of "Surviving" Funds 1990–1999	760	
Total # of "Surviving" Funds 2000–2009		1,847

Myth #3
Market Timing Works

Market timing is defined as any attempt to alter or change the mix of assets, based on a prediction—or forecast—of the future. The myth that this can be done consistently and predictably is as pervasive as it is false. Granted, sometimes a prognosticator of future events is occasionally right, just like those folks who read tea leaves or Tarot cards. But you will have the same measure of success dealing with the latter as you will depending on those who claim to possess the ability to consistently foresee the future of the stock market and know when to buy or sell. Regardless of the means by which they may claim to have this prescience, the numbers suggest otherwise.

Before we do the math and science on this one, let me pose this question: If someone did possess that ability, wouldn't he or she be wealthy and famous beyond measure? Sure. The other day I read a newspaper column's clever jab at the lottery: "What is the lottery?" asked the columnist. "It's a tax on the people who cannot do math." But then don't we pick up the same paper occasionally to see a photograph of a lottery winner, holding up a check the size of a garage door for $40 million? Just because they get it right once, even twice, does not mean that it springs from anything except blind chance, does it? What borders on the criminal is the attempt of professional money managers to convince us that they have the power to "win the lottery" for us with our portfolios.

Perhaps the most salient indictment against such claims is the data published by DALBAR, whose research serves as a kind of *Consumer Reports* of the investments industry. While Morningstar looks at the *actual returns* of funds, DALBAR is an independent research firm that does massive studies on Investor Behavior—the *real results* that investors get. In 2008, DALBAR concluded a twenty-year study of tens of thousands of brokerage accounts for investors who have over $100,000 invested. Here's what they found:

- During the time period, the S&P 500 Index returned 8.64%.
- The average equity fund investor's return during the same period was only 1.87%.
- The systematic equity fund investor did a little better at 2.70% because they were buying a set amount periodically whether the market was down or up.
- And how about the *market timer?* What were their results? NEGATIVE –0.83%.

So what was the reason for the gap? What was the investor behavior that contributed to such disastrous results? The average investor:

- Carelessly chases "hot" asset categories
- Inadvertently forsakes diversification
- Often panics and takes money out of the market during periods of volatility, attempting to time the market
- Sells asset categories that are low and buys asset categories that are high.
- Without a coach, the vast majority of investors shoot themselves in the foot because they lack the *knowledge* to set realistic investment expectations and the *discipline* to maintain a strategy over the long-term.

What would have prevented it? Following four simple rules would have gone a long way:

1. Own equities and fixed income assets.
2. Diversify among the equity asset categories.
3. Periodically rebalance your portfolio. (Buy asset categories in the portfolio that are relatively low and sell categories that are relatively high)
4. Stay disciplined. You're in it for the long haul.

The problem with trying to time the market is that you need to be right twice. You need to bail out at just the right time, and you need to get back in at just the right time. The truth is, nobody has been able to do it successfully and consistently, ever.

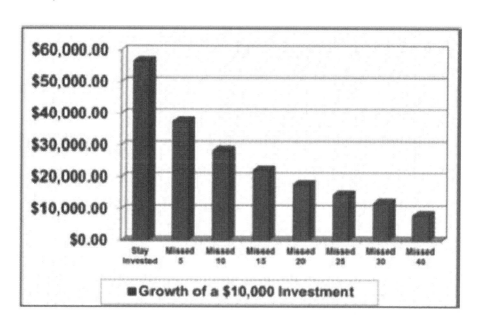

Can chasing the right time to jump in and out of the market in an effort to "beat" the market take its toll? Consider the chart shown here. It shows how a $10,000 investment would have fared had the investor *missed* the market's top-performing days over the twenty-year period from January 1, 1991, to December 31, 2010. The investor who simply stayed put for the entire period would have accumulated $56,561, whereas just missing the ten top-performing days would have left the investor accumulating only $28,288, about half as much.

A word of caution: These days you may encounter the term "tactical asset allocation" used by some portfolio managers. The idea is that it is possible to rebalance a percentage of assets held in various categories in order to take advantage of what they call "market pricing anomalies." But this still leaves the "experts" handling your money with the obligation to make a prediction about which way the market will move. They will decide, based on this prediction, which part of your portfolio pie is underweight or overweight. Again, the truth is that this is just a clever rephrasing of "market timing." Run!

Myth #4
The Cost of Investing
(Or...What You Don't See Won't Hurt You)

Money managers who make commissions buying and selling within your portfolio will be uncomfortable with this, but fees incurred by investors to buy, sell, and own stocks or mutual funds can, and often do, hurt you.

Let's say you call up your broker and say, "I have a hundred shares of XYZ fund I want to sell. What is the price per share I can get for them right now?"

Broker: "You can get $49.50 per share"

"Did I say, sell? I meant buy. What can I buy a hundred shares in XYZ fund for?"

Broker: "You can buy them for $50.00 per share"

Wait a minute! You mean there is a difference between the price of the shares, depending upon whether I am buying or selling? Yep. It's called the bid/ask spread cost. In the parlance of mutual funds, the difference in the buy and sell price is called the "spread." If it's on the New York Stock Exchange, the person telling you that is called the "specialist." If you were in Las Vegas, it would be called the "house." In Las Vegas, the casinos do not care if you are playing cards or the slot machines, as long as you are playing. That way, the "house" always makes its cut. That's how they build those giant hotels.

Do not go looking for this information in the prospectus of the mutual fund, by the way. It is not there. The cost of this is not captured by the expense ratio of the mutual fund. And if you are trading shares in the market, it doesn't matter whether you are an individual investor or a giant fund, you will still pay this fee. If you are trading large-cap stocks such as Exxon Mobil, it is a pretty small amount. But if the transactions involve small-cap or micro-cap companies such as Advanced Battery Technologies, it drives your trading fees up a considerable amount.

What about "no load" mutual funds? Does this apply to them? The bid/ask spread has nothing to do with the sales charge on the fund itself. It has nothing to do with the expense ratio of the fund. This is an internal drag on the returns of the funds that the manager has to accommodate each time there is a transaction. The point is that the more active a fund manager is when it comes to trading, the more cost there is associated with the actual returns that filter down to the individual investor. It may be swept under the carpet as a cost of doing business. That's fine when the market is up, and the fund is making you money. It's not so fine when the costs continue even though the fund is taking a beating. Would it surprise you to know that there are some pretty big mutual funds out there that are also "market makers," who make the spread on top of the customary fees charged by the fund itself?

The truth is, most investors have no idea how much active management is costing them. One recently published study by Kenneth French, "The Cost of Active Investing," compared the cost of active versus passive investments.[7] The author of the study concluded that active investors, a designation that includes the vast majority, could have increased their average annual return by .067% over the 1980-2006 period, by just switching from an active to a passive portfolio. Trying to beat the markets cost investors approximately $80 billion a year, the study concluded. That is a pretty expensive price tag for believing that new and unknowable information can be the possession of only a chosen few who have the unique ability to consistently predict the future movements of a market that is erratic by its very nature.

Explicit Fees

Implicit Fees

7   French, Kenneth R. "Presidential Address: The Cost of Active Investing." *The Journal of Finance* (2008): 1537-573.

At its roots, the problem is not with Wall Street and the massive propaganda machine that perpetuates these myths, because it is in the best interests of the financial barons to have them believed. The problem is with the ill-informed public that simply does not raise enough questions. To be fair, however, it is more likely a case of not knowing what questions to ask.

What you don't know CAN hurt you

On July 16, 1999, John F. Kennedy, Jr. took off in his Piper Saratoga single-engine airplane on his way from New Jersey to Martha's Vineyard, a flight that would end in disaster for him and his beautiful, young wife. He was licensed to fly the aircraft but had not received his instrument rating. There were several factors that caused the crash, but this one single deficit probably cost him his life, as well as the lives of all those with him. In the darkening haze, Kennedy was unable to make out the coastline below and became disoriented. The instrument training would have allowed him to navigate the plane safely out of the haze and make a safe landing.

It was not that flying the airplane was necessarily dangerous. He had logged hundreds of hours and was fully licensed for visual flight rules. But that did him little good when he gazed at the panel full of instruments and couldn't understand them.

Kennedy would have no doubt given any portion of his substantial wealth to have had a copilot who knew how to read the dials and numbers and guide him safely back down. In the investigation that followed the crash, there were those who sought to place blame somewhere. Who had allowed him to take off in worsening weather conditions? Was he given no weather briefing? Did someone approve his flight plan without examining the status of his training and experience? As it turns out, under the conditions of his flight, he was not required to file a flight plan. His flight instructor did not know that he would be flying in those conditions without an instructor on board. Some have blamed Kennedy's own hubris for what happened, but that is unfair. He simply didn't know what he didn't know.

Investing can be complicated. The haze that is thrown at us by the environment of the financial world can have a dizzying effect if we do not have the proper navigational tools and know how to use them. We can get lost in the fog of conflicting opinions put forth by magazines, commercials, the Internet, and the talking heads on television. But, as is so often the case, worse than not knowing, is not knowing that we need to know.

I view my role in helping people make financial decisions as that of a coach. In athletics, a coach doesn't perform the athletes' job; he teaches them how to do it better. The coach doesn't throw the ball or swim the lane. The coach's job is to observe the athlete throw the ball or swim the lane and point out techniques that can better equip the athlete for the task at hand. Financial coaches teach clients practical skills and techniques to manage their money on a daily basis. Clients learn to plan ahead, deal with daily money decisions, and generate solutions to reach financial goals.

Just as good doctors will spend time listening to their patients and asking the pertinent questions before making a diagnosis, financial coaches will listen and ask questions of their clients to determine what they wish to accomplish with their wealth. A good doctor is part scientist, part counselor and part healer. Good doctors will not prescribe medicine indiscriminately on the *chance* that it will make the patient better. When they take the Hippocratic Oath, doctors promise to "do no harm."

It's the same with investing. There is no silver bullet when it comes to wealth building, wealth preservation, and income planning. There is no magic potion and there is no wonder drug. For financial coaches, to "do no harm" means that they will do their best to educate their clients—with math, science, and solid fact, not chancy predictions or fanciful scenarios—so the clients know what they face and can prepare for it. This is especially applicable to baby boomers who are on the threshold of retirement. They likely have been saving for this new phase of their lives for many years. How criminal it would be to steer them in a direction that could cause them to experience unexpected losses right at the moment their money is needed for retirement!

Occasionally I will fire myself as someone's financial coach if they are determined to proceed with a strategy that I know will lead to dismal consequences. It is not that I do not wish to help them. I just cannot accept professional responsibility for their reckless course.

A good coach builds the client's confidence in his/her own strengths, ideas, and solutions. Financial coaching is an ongoing process to teach and guide clients as they learn to make conscious choices about their financial lives, and develop a plan of action to improve their financial well-being.

I believe that the time has come to rethink how we approach our retirement. With the phasing out of the traditional pension plans, increasing market volatility, increasing debt levels, and the devaluing of our currency, our world is changing rapidly. Consequently, avoiding a big mistake with our retirement assets is more crucial than ever.

We are living longer than we ever have, with retirements extending out thirty-plus years. You need to take the necessary steps to put a financial plan in place. In the following chapters, I will walk you through the process of constructing a retirement portfolio made to last throughout your lifetime.

So once again, here are the myths of investing that have wrapped themselves around the investing minds of most people like unwanted ivy.

The Myths
- **Stock Selection Works**
- **Track Record Investing Works**
- **Market Timing Works**
- **Costs of Investing Don't Matter**

As important as it is to know the myths of investing, it is vital that we know the truth. If the myths don't work, then what does?

CHAPTER SIX

Working with a Free Market Portfolio System

*"Underlying most arguments against the free market
is a lack of belief in freedom itself."*
– Milton Friedman

The Free Market Portfolio Theory is an investment approach that is grounded in over fifty years of academic research—math, science, and statistics. Let me caution you, it is not glitzy or glamorous. It is actually kind of "engineering boring." It involves no circus-act shenanigans like the guy on TV with the funny hat tossing out stock tips. It springs from research and statistics and is put together by some of the best minds in the world, and they are not selling anything or attempting to play on your emotions. The reason why Free Market Portfolio Theory (FMPT) works is because it is all about numbers and probability and not about getting lucky.

The FMPT is a disciplined approach to capturing market returns while managing volatility. It is made up of three academic components:

1. Free markets work
2. The three-factor model
3. The modern portfolio theory

The people behind the FMPT are several leaders of the academic economic world, two of whom are Nobel Prize winners, all of whom are highly recognized by academia for what they do. They include:

- **Harry Markowitz:**
  Nobel Prize Laureate, 1990, University of Chicago
- **Merton H. Miller:**
  Nobel Prize Laureate, 1990, Robert R. McCormick Distinguished Service, University of Chicago
- **Rex Sinquefield:**
  Coauthor *Stocks, Bonds, Bills, and Inflation*, MBA, University of Chicago, BA, St. Louis University
- **Roger G. Ibbotson:**
  Coauthor *Stocks, Bonds, Bills, and Inflation*, Professor of Finance, School of Organization and Management, Yale University
- **Eugene F. Fama:**
  Robert R. McCormick Distinguished Service Professor, Graduate School of Business, University of Chicago
- **Kenneth French:**
  Professor of Finance at the Tuck School of Business, Dartmouth College

As impressive as that list is, I am even more impressed by whose names do not appear here. No television personalities and no CEOs of big Wall Street firms who get fat bonuses for perpetuating the myths we described in the previous chapter. These are professors who have no reason to deceive and no ulterior motive. Professors, after all, are paid to teach. If they teach economics, they are trained to collect the data and analyze it and come up with verifiable conclusions. So with that as a backdrop, let's examine their work one component at a time and, having "checked our opinions at the door," let's decide if FMPT holds up.

Free Markets Work

Please meet Eugene Francis "Gene" Fama (born February 14, 1939), an American economist, known for his work on portfolio theory and asset pricing, both theoretical and empirical. He is currently Robert R. McCormick Distinguished Service Professor of Finance at the University Of Chicago Booth School Of Business. Fama, who has spent his entire teaching career at the University of Chicago, developed the "Free Markets Work" component of the theory in 1965 and made this comment in his PhD dissertation in that year: *"In an efficient market at any point in time, the actual price of a security will be a good estimate of its intrinsic value."*

That statement is so profoundly simple, you have to read it twice to get it. In other words, stock prices are probably worth what they are selling for at any given time. But wait a minute—that puts the stock pickers and market timers in the same category as snake oil salesmen! Yes, Dr. Fama does precisely that.

Fama got his first taste of the world of finance when he worked for a stock market newsletter company in Boston while he attended Tufts University. He was hired to observe the market and locate signals that would tell investors when to buy and sell stocks. As time passed, however, he grew more and more frustrated because he found out how impossible it was to accurately predict market trends. These indicators he was hired to find were simply bogus.

After receiving his doctorate at Chicago Booth University, Fama published his dissertation, titled "The Behavior of Stock Market Prices" in the 1965 issue of the *Journal of Business*. That work was subsequently rewritten into a less technical article, "Random Walks in Stock Market Prices," which is what he is best known for today. His PhD dissertation concluded that stock price movements are unpredictable subject to influence by events. His article "The Adjustment of Stock Prices to New Information" in the *International Economic Review*, 1969 (with several coauthors), was the first study of its kind that sought to analyze how stock prices respond to events.

TWO VIEWS OF MARKETS

Random price movements ←——— ———→ Predictable price movements

MARKETS WORK

The Markets Work hypothesis sees the market as random and unpredictable. Amazingly, the randomness of the market actually indicates that prices quickly and accurately reflect information.

MARKETS FAIL

The Markets Fail premise presumes that prices react to information slowly enough to allow some individuals to analyze and predict the future.

Fama is most often thought of as the father of efficient market hypothesis (EMH), which asserts that financial markets are "informationally efficient." In other words, since information about publicly traded securities is available to everyone at about the same time, it is impossible to beat the markets consistently without purchasing riskier investments. Even so-called insider information will wash out in the outworking of the market's natural function.

Fama contends that efforts to beat the market through technical analysis and studying charts and graphs are of no avail since they also ultimately collide with this natural barrier built into a free market system.

Wait a minute! Does that mean that back in the 1960s he was telling those in the securities industry that their sales pitch was bogus? That their assertion of being able to pick stocks that would do well for their clients and beat the market had no basis in scientific fact? So it appears. Others had, of course, run the idea up the flagpole of public opinion, but Fama was the first one to prove it with the numbers after a tremendous amount of arduous research.

The Three-Factor Model

Factor 1: The Market Factor
Factor 2: The Size Factor
Factor 3: The "Value" Factor

Eugene Fama
&
Kenneth French

Source: Fama, Eugene F., and Kenneth R. French, 1992 "The cross-section of Expected Stock Returns", Journal of Finance 47 (June), 427-465

The Three-Factor Model

In the early 1990s, Fama teamed up with the much-younger Kenneth French to collaborate on several economic papers that gained national recognition. In 1992, they sought to determine the factors that explain the relationship between investment risk and return for stocks. The idea was that if it could be known precisely what factors in a portfolio accounted for returns, then a portfolio could be built around that data. It would have the effect of maximizing returns while being adequately compensated for the level of risk taken. This model is highly significant. Understanding it will allow you to change the way you invest. Instead of following the myths of investing already debunked here and by so many in economic academia, your investments can be based on the same sound research that is used by the most sophisticated investment advisors to invest trillions of dollars of assets.

The traditional asset pricing model, known formally as the capital asset pricing model, CAPM, uses only one variable, beta, to describe the returns of a portfolio or stock with the returns of the market as a whole. In contrast, the Fama–French model uses three variables. Fama and French started with the observation that two classes of stocks have tended to do better than the market as a whole.

There may be critics of the three-factor model developed by Fama and French, but the proof is in the proverbial pudding. The three factors that make up the model are:

1. The market factor: The extra risk of stocks versus fixed income
2. The size factor: The extra risk of small-cap stocks over large-cap stocks
3. The value factor: The extra risk of high book-to-market (BTM) over low BTM stocks

A portfolio's exposure to these three basic but diverse risk factors can determine the vast majority of investment results. The three-factor model is extremely useful in portfolios to determine how many equity positions to hold, the allocation between small and large equities and the allocation between value and growth equities.

The Free Market Mindset

I am a big believer in the free market system. A free market system is one that allows the free and unencumbered trading by interested parties of goods, services, equities, securities, bonds, and currencies without interference. As is the case with any social structure, however, there is the possibility for misuse. Governments can then serve as referees, but only to the point that they make sure the rules are fair—equally applied and adhered to. That is why we have insider trading laws and fraud protection provisions. But over manipulation kills the goose that lays the golden eggs.

A free market mindset recognizes that the stock market, the media, and popular culture encourage behavior consistent with the belief that the market is inefficient. Without a clearly defined investment philosophy, it is easy to be manipulated by media, advertisers, and investment professionals eager to sell products. It is necessary to understand that there is a choice to be made about how you believe the market works. If you believe the market is inherently efficient, and that market forces will eventually correct any listing of the keel to port or starboard, then your investment strategy will reflect that, and those principles will safely guide you through any storm. When it comes to investing, your *strategy* has to agree with your *belief system* or it will not work. At least it will not work long term. And when it comes to your belief system, you either believe in the free market or you don't. If you do not believe that free markets work, then you believe that markets consistently misprice goods and services. Therefore, it would be reasonable (if that were true) and possible to take advantage of the mispricing and pass value on to the investor by increasing returns and avoiding losses in investments.

On the other hand, if you believe that free market system is the best determinant of market prices and that all available information is factored into the current price, then only new and unknowable information and events change pricing into the future. You also believe that the randomness of the market makes it impossible for any individual or entity to consistently predict market movements and capture additional returns unrelated to risk.

There are people in both camps. Some think the market is efficient and others that it is inefficient. Most people (specifically investors), have never given it much thought. As an investor, it is extremely important for you to define this belief structure for yourself.

I once heard it said that thinking is hard work, which explains why so few people engage in it. It is true that most investors will simply use the latest investment strategy, or the one their neighbor used successfully. But I know that once you are clear about what you truly believe, it will tell you how you need to manage your money.

Modern Portfolio Theory

This basic component of Free Market Portfolio Theory is the Modern Portfolio Theory, which earned the Nobel Prize in Economics in 1990 for the collaborative work of Harry Markowitz, Merton Miller, and Myron Scholes.

The basic idea is that the risk of an individual asset is far less important than the contribution the asset makes to the portfolio's risk as a whole. The Modern Portfolio Theory holds that, for the same amount of risk, diversification can increase returns. Since the mechanics to reduce risk is dissimilar price movements, the task to be accomplished in designing a portfolio appropriate to the MPT is to find assets with low correlations.

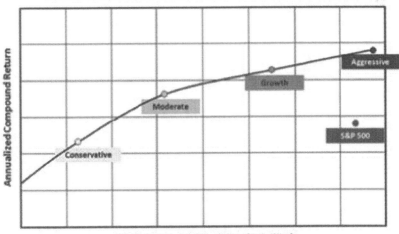

MARKOWITZ EFFICIENT FRONTIER
Maximizing Expected Returns for Any Level of Volatility

Meet Dr. Harry Markowitz, the pioneer of the Modern Portfolio Theory. It is interesting that his doctorate paper, the one that led to his Nobel Prize, was written in 1952, but the prize was not awarded until 1990. Why? Because it took nearly forty years for computer technology to advance to the point where his theories could be proven...but proven they were. The time lapse between his work and his recognition for it is reminiscent of that of Albert Einstein, who reportedly wrote his black hole theory on the back of an envelope. But it was not until forty years later that a black hole was actually discovered in space by the Hubble telescope. Mr. Markowitz, like Einstein, was truly ahead of his time in figuring out how to use the financial math concept he called the "Efficient Frontier" as a reliable way to look at risk and return.

The illustration above is an example of the Markowitz Efficient Frontier. It is a hypothetical graph that illustrates an optimal portfolio return for any given level of risk. For example, we can take an investor who has 100% of his or her money in the S&P 500 and say, you have a historical rate of return of around 10%, and you have a historical volatility of around 19%.

If you are comfortable with that level of return, why don't we move you straight across this graph to pick up essentially the same return with one half of the volatility? Or, if you are comfortable with that volatility, we can just move you straight up the graph, pick up an extra 2–3% rate of return per year without any additional volatility in your portfolio. Using what is called the free market investment analysis, now a financial professional is able to plot where a client's current investment portfolio falls on the Markowitz Efficient Frontier.

So how do we create an optimal portfolio, considering that we do not want to employ traditional investment strategies that involve the investing myths previously proven untrue? Asset allocation is the key. In 1986, a study titled "Determinants of Portfolio Performance" was conducted and published by G.P. Brinson, L.R. Hood, and G.L. Beebower, which should have forever changed the way you look at investing. Unfortunately, few have heard of it. This study found that the asset allocation of a portfolio—that is, the division between stocks, bonds, and cash—is the primary determinant (causal factor) of why returns in a portfolio vary. These researchers contend that their findings show that stock picking and market timing are, for the most part, irrelevant to portfolio performance, even though this is most likely what most brokers focus on. The determinants study points the arrow of focus clearly toward asset allocation instead. The study shows that 91.5% of a portfolio's ROI, or return on investment, is gained through the appropriate allocation of the asset classes it contains. The proper mix will make for good returns. An imbalance and a lack of diversification will result in poor performance. So the modern investor need not worry about which individual stock he or she owns, but rather, how each type of security is represented in the portfolio, and how these investments work together.

Asset Class Correlation

Another term you will encounter in understanding the Modern Portfolio Theory is "correlation." Correlation is the relationship between two investments. Let's take a look at how similarly or dissimilarly they behave in the market. Sometimes in the classes I conduct on this from our Michigan offices, I like to ask the students to finish a sentence for me: "If you want extra return in your investment portfolio, then you have to take more what?" Invariably the answer I get is "risk." I get this answer because that has been the traditional pitch of those who make money on your risk taking. The data provided by the clear-thinking Markowitz supports the idea that, instead of taking more risk, you play off the correlation of one asset class with another. In this strategy, what we are looking for are assets with dissimilar price movements, so that when one goes down, the other has a strong potential of offsetting it with an upward period. One goes down; the other goes up.

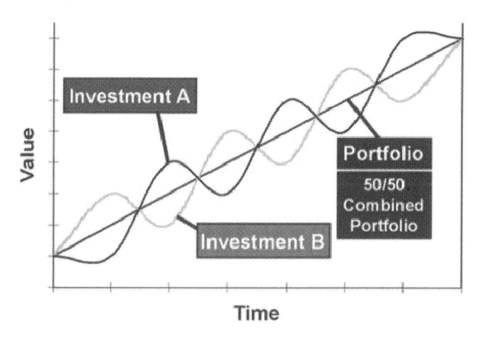

Dr. Markowitz measured the likelihood of various asset categories moving dissimilarly. It is possible to have two assets that, by themselves, look fairly volatile, but when you combine them in this way in a portfolio, you actually increase the rate of return and reduce the volatility. The result is just what baby boomers need to maneuver through the dangers of investing at this new phase of their lives: *performance* and *safety*. Knowing and understanding the correlation of assets within a portfolio, then is the cornerstone of diversification.

How to Use Correlation

The goal is to increase returns and lower volatility, right? We do that through working with the correlation of the asset categories. The lower the correlation between two asset categories, the less similar they are. We will run into another term in this process, so we might as well introduce it now: standard deviation.

Standard deviation is widely used to measure variability. It shows how much dispersion exists from the average, or mean, or expected value of something. For example, the margin of error in polling data is determined by calculating the expected *standard deviation* in the results if the same poll were to be conducted multiple times. That way, they can determine accuracy. In finance, the standard deviation on a rate of return on an investment measures the volatility. If we can understand it, and predict it, then we can contain and control it.

All you have to do is remember that standard deviation is a form of volatility. The higher the standard deviation number, the higher the volatility.

Let's say that forty years ago we put together a portfolio using just the S&P Index, and we invested 100% in large US stocks. We would have had an average return of about 11.75%. Our standard deviation, or volatility factor, would be about 18%.

Now let's go back and diversify. Let's take 30% and put it in a large international stock index, the EAFE (the acronym stands for Europe, Australasia and Far East). So now we have 70% in the S&P 500 and 30% in the EAFE. An interesting thing happens. We actually *increase* our return to 12.16% and we *reduce* our volatility by a few basis points.

Now let's continue the diversification process. Let's take 10% and put it into a small international index. Our volatility remains low, about fifteen basis points less than our original portfolio.

Basis Points: 100 basis points = 1%, so 50 BPs = 0.50%

Our returns, however, are a few basis points higher than before. So with this remarkably simple hypothetical example, we've been able to add almost 1% return to the portfolio, with no additional volatility over the same period of time.

Using the Three-Factor Model

When Kenneth French and Eugene Fama first began working on this model, they had no number of factors in mind. They merely wanted to narrow down which sources of risk the market systematically rewarded. They narrowed them down to market, size, and value.

- The Market Factor—This one is pretty straightforward, really. It tells us that it is riskier to invest in the stock market than it is in fixed-income instruments, like bonds, cash, or CDs. But because there is more risk involved, stocks provide a higher rate of return than fixed income instruments.

- The Size Factor—Small companies are riskier than large companies. Yes, they give a larger expected rate of return than large companies, because there is more risk involved.

- The Value Factor—This factor refers to the extra risk exposure, and the extra risk premium, of investing in high-book-to-market-value stocks. Value stocks are companies that have a lower market price than other companies relative to their size. These companies are usually experiencing some type of financial distress—perhaps they have experienced some bad publicity—and usually their earnings are down. Therefore, they are riskier but offer a higher potential return to investors.

So what does the three-factor model tell us? Simply that the market rewards investors for taking risks, especially in equities, a little bit more for small companies, and even a little bit more return for distressed companies. But the statistics that we are able to compile using this model allow us to define the relationship between risk and return. It makes it possible to calculate expected returns based on these risk factors. And, as stated before, if we can understand the information and track it, we can use it to make decisions in portfolio design that will allow us to fare much better than the nonscientific approach of guessing, attempting to foretell the future, and relying on the traditional myths of investing.

> "Money, if it does not bring you happiness, will at least help you be miserable in comfort."
> - Helen Gurley Brown

FACTOR 1: THE MARKET FACTOR

- **Equities are riskier than fixed income.**
- **Equities historically provide a higher rate of return.**

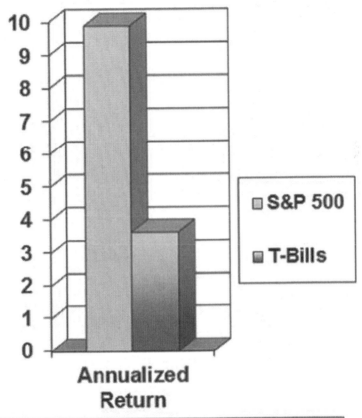

1926–2011	S&P 500	T-Bills
Annualized Return	9.78	3.57
Standard Deviation	20.29	3.12

FACTOR 2: THE SIZE FACTOR

- **Small companies are riskier than large companies.**
- **Small companies historically provide a higher return than large companies.**

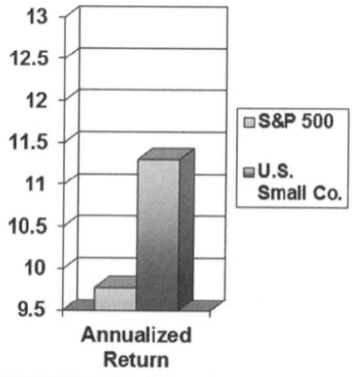

1926–2011	S&P 500	U.S. Small Co.
Annualized Return	9.78	11.31
Standard Deviation	20.29	30.71

FACTOR 3: THE VALUE FACTOR

- **High book-to-market (value) stocks are riskier than low book-to-market (growth) stocks.**
- **High book-to-market stocks historically provide higher return than low book-to-market stocks.**

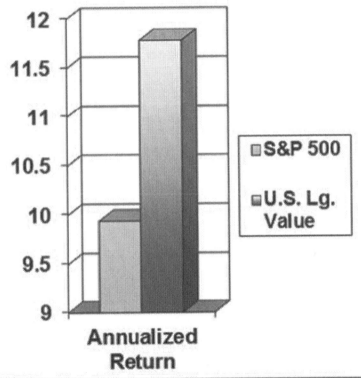

Annualized Return

July 1926–2011	S&P 500	U.S. Lg. Value
Annualized Return	9.85	11.54
Standard Deviation	19.18	25.19

ALLOCATION OF SAMPLE ASSET CLASS MIXES

ASSET CLASSES	HYPOTHETICAL MIX	SAMPLE ASSET CLASS MIXES Percent of Portfolio			
		CONSERVATIVE	MODERATE	GROWTH	AGGRESSIVE
FIXED INCOME					
Cash Equivalents	3.04%	2.00%	2.00%	2.00%	2.00%
Short Term Fixed	0.00%	36.50%	24.00%	11.50%	1.50%
Intermediate Term Bonds	0.00%	36.50%	24.00%	11.50%	1.50%
Long Term Bonds	0.00%	0.0%	0.0%	0.0%	0.0%
Sub Total Fixed Income	3.04%	75.00%	50.00%	25.00%	5.00%
U.S. EQUITY					
Large Stocks	86.21%	2.63%	4.50%	6.37%	7.50%
Large Value Stocks	0.00%	5.25%	9.00%	12.75%	15.00%
Small Stocks	0.00%	5.26%	9.00%	12.75%	15.00%
Small Value Stocks	0.00%	4.38%	7.50%	10.63%	12.50%
Sub Total U.S. Equity	86.21%	17.50%	30.00%	42.50%	50.00%
INTERNATIONAL EQUITY					
Large Stocks	10.76%	2.63%	7.0%	11.38%	15.75%
Small Stocks	0.00%	4.85%	13.00%	21.12%	29.25%
Sub Total Int'l Equity	10.76%	7.50%	20.00%	32.50%	45.00%
GRAND TOTAL	100.00%	100%	100%	100%	100%

HISTORICAL INVESTMENT MARKET PERFORMANCE OF SAMPLE ASSET CLASS MIXES

This illustration shows the annual rate of return for certain hypothetical asset class mixes based on the performance of various market indices and index mutual funds. The intent of this chart is to show the benefits of diversification into several asset classes with low or negative correlation among the selected asset classes.

YEAR	HYPOTHETICAL MIX	CONSERVATIVE	MODERATE	GROWTH	AGGRESSIVE
1973	-13.96%	0.23%	-5.91%	-12.07%	-16.79%
1974	-24.95%	1.50%	-7.28%	-16.06%	-20.35%
1975	36.25%	13.20%	30.06%	40.53%	49.33%
1976	21.17%	17.02%	21.38%	25.75%	28.27%
1977	-3.94%	8.76%	16.15%	23.52%	30.52%
1978	9.55%	11.31%	18.27%	26.32%	31.55%
1979	16.86%	13.99%	15.58%	17.17%	17.66%
1980	30.96%	14.87%	20.96%	23.94%	27.00%
1981	-3.90%	17.42%	13.32%	9.21%	5.68%
1982	18.69%	21.01%	20.72%	18.46%	15.98%
1983	22.37%	14.59%	20.63%	24.67%	31.47%
1984	6.55%	9.22%	8.66%	7.96%	7.59%
1985	34.07%	23.83%	30.47%	38.10%	45.02%
1986	23.64%	18.80%	23.28%	29.73%	36.11%
1987	7.26%	5.44%	8.00%	10.56%	13.60%
1988	17.75%	11.91%	16.28%	21.06%	24.96%
1989	28.56%	13.71%	16.00%	19.29%	21.98%
1990	-4.90%	2.91%	-4.24%	-11.98%	-17.16%
1991	27.75%	16.26%	18.97%	21.66%	23.08%
1992	8.41%	7.88%	4.96%	6.15%	4.61%
1993	12.97%	10.87%	16.11%	21.36%	25.87%
1994	2.12%	0.30%	1.71%	3.06%	4.51%
1995	33.81%	12.92%	15.63%	18.34%	19.77%
1996	20.64%	8.86%	9.75%	11.15%	11.66%
1997	29.14%	8.32%	10.48%	11.66%	11.61%
1998	26.87%	6.74%	8.15%	9.61%	10.88%
1999	21.32%	7.83%	12.20%	16.06%	20.45%
2000	-9.17%	8.27%	2.80%	0.39%	-2.09%
2001	-12.41%	5.41%	2.96%	0.52%	-2.19%
2002	-20.69%	2.03%	3.13%	-8.29%	-12.11%
2003	28.98%	14.19%	26.42%	38.06%	48.54%
2004	11.64%	6.69%	12.07%	17.46%	21.97%
2005	5.83%	4.07%	7.15%	10.23%	12.98%
2006	16.85%	9.07%	13.80%	18.03%	22.46%
2007	6.13%	4.06%	3.64%	3.22%	3.19%
2008	-38.48%	-0.39%	-17.31%	-29.23%	-38.97%
2009	26.31%	10.50%	19.58%	28.67%	36.06%
2010	13.87%	7.02%	11.04%	15.05%	18.16%
2011	0.54%	-0.60%	-3.58%	-4.57%	-9.17%
Annualized Return	9.56%	9.18%	10.60%	11.87%	12.58%
Standard Deviation	17.56	6.49	10.56	15.41	19.58

Past performance is no guarantee of future results and investors may experience a loss. 39 Year Performance figures taken from Dimensional Fund Advisor, Inc. (DFA) Returns software 12/11. Some data provided to DFA by the Center for Research & Security Pricing(CRSP), University of Chicago. Portfolio net of all fees.

PART TWO

Bullet-Proof Your Portfolio For the Long Haul

CHAPTER SEVEN

Asset Allocation Is Priority #1

"Risk comes from not knowing what you are doing."
— **Warren Buffet**

Over the years, I have developed into quite a critic of television commercials. The ones I despise most feature the loud talkers. Whoever produces these irritating spots must have been brought up in a family where the one who could talk the loudest always won the argument. I'm also not a big fan of the commercials that try to get you to notice their products by using celebrities, either. Who cares what kind of underwear some famous basketball player wears? The ones I like the most, however, are the ones that make you think. They make their point with cleverness, and sometimes a touch of the absurd, just so you will pay attention.

One of my favorites is aired by the insurance company, ING, which is famous for the park bench, which has become their trademark. The ING commercials are always low key and intellectual. The one I like best opens with a man walking his dog. Under the man's right arm is what looks like a large number made out of Styrofoam and painted orange. The number is hard to make out, but you can tell that it is over $1 million. The dog walker is casually carrying this oversized number down the street, when he encounters a neighbor on a ladder trimming a hedge. The neighbor, too, has a large Styrofoam "number" perched beside him atop the hedge, only his is in sparkly purple, and reads "$Gazillion."

The inference is that everyone has a certain number that they need to accumulate, so they can retire and still live life comfortably. The man walking his dog has an exact number in mind. He, of course, is the smart one because he knows his number. He has taken the time to think out what his expenses will be in retirement. He has accounted for such contingencies as inflation, health-care costs, etc. He has come up with an exact number. The hedge trimmer has nothing but a vague idea of what he needs to accumulate before he retires. In the commercial, he even admits that his plan is just to throw some money at his "Gazillion" and see what happens.

The company presents the message brilliantly: if you fail to plan, you are likely to fail, and that guessing about retirement is not the way to go. But if I were writing the script for the commercial, I don't think I would have made the dog walker's number quite so high (I told you I was a critic). Many of my clients are fortunate enough to retire with over a million dollars, but from the sampling I have done over the years, it is a bit out of range for a number of retirees. Unless your lifestyle is lavish, you can get by with less, especially if you are careful with your budgeting once you are in the "home stretch."

When it comes to investing our nest egg, it is important to stay on safe ground. After all, we are not dealing with play money here. Our "number" probably represents what we have painstakingly tucked away for our future. So conservation of those assets should become our mantra as we look for ways to put it to work and make it grow. One way to do that is through proper asset allocation.

Simply defined, asset allocation is an investment strategy that attempts to balance risk versus reward by adjusting the percentage of each asset in an investment portfolio according to the investor's risk tolerance, goals, and investment time frame. The way to invest intelligently is by making use of several asset classes at once and by properly diversifying. As soon as the phrase "asset allocation" pops up, most people immediately think of the idiom: "Never put all your eggs in one basket." That is, of course, the point. No one quite knows the origin of eggs/basket idiom, but the meaning is obvious: do not rely on one thing too heavily, in case it goes wrong. If you put all your eggs in one basket and you accidentally drop the basket, every egg gets broken. If you had used two baskets, you would at least still have some eggs left, even if you had dropped one of the baskets.

In investing, asset allocation has to do with which assets are owned and in what proportion. It involves spreading one's risk by putting assets in several different investment categories, or diversification. This way, the fall in value of one asset class does not ruin the entire portfolio if it is properly balanced.

I grew up in the village of Clarkston, Michigan, located about thirty miles north of Detroit. It was small enough to have individually owned hardware stores, and I noticed as a boy that the owners of the store would put certain items out on the sidewalk in front of the store each morning. I remember think-ing, even at that age, that the sidewalk wares were placed there for a purpose. When snow was in the forecast, there would be a rack of sleds out front, and perhaps shovels on display. If rain was in the forecast, a barrel of umbrellas stood near the entrance. This was smart marketing, I concluded. It also advertised the fact that a trip inside the store could yield just about anything you needed for just about any purpose. There was variety here. On days when sunglasses didn't move, umbrellas would. If the umbrellas and the sunglasses didn't move, then maybe it was a good day for the snow shovels. This way, the store could reduce the risk of losing money on any given day.

Asset allocation involves dividing an investment portfolio among different asset categories, such as stocks, bonds, and cash. The process of determining which mix of assets to hold in your portfolio is a highly personal one. The asset allocation that works best for you at any given point in your life will depend largely on your *time horizon* and your ability to tolerate *risk*.

Risk and reward are inextricably entwined when it comes to investing. The expression "no pain, no gain" probably originated in the athletic community. I can tell you from personal experi-ence that running until you feel you can't run any longer, and then pushing for one more block, or one more tenth of a mile, is the way to train the body for the rigors of a foot race. And "no pain, no gain" comes close to summing up the relation-ship between risk and reward, too. Don't let anyone tell you otherwise: All investments involve some degree of risk. If you intend to purchases securities—such as stocks, bonds, or mutual funds—it is essential that you understand before you invest that losses are possible.

The reward for taking on risk is the potential for a greater investment return. If you have a financial goal with a long time horizon, you are likely to make more money by carefully investing in asset categories with greater risk, like stocks or bonds, rather than restricting your investments to assets with less risk, like cash equivalents. On the other hand, investing solely in cash investments may be appropriate for short-term financial goals.

Investment Choices

A vast array of investment products exists, including stocks and stock mutual funds, corporate and municipal bonds, bond mutual funds, lifecycle funds, exchange-traded funds, money market funds, and US Treasury securities. For many financial goals, investing in a mix of stocks, bonds, and cash can be an appropriate strategy. Let's take a closer look at the characteristics of the three major asset categories.

Stocks have historically had the greatest risk and highest returns among the three major asset categories. As an asset category, stocks are a portfolio's "heavy hitter," offering the greatest potential for growth. Stocks hit home runs, but also strike out. The volatility of stocks makes them a decidedly risky investment in the short term. Large company stocks as a group, for example, have lost money on average about one out of every three years. And sometimes the losses have been quite dramatic. But investors willing to ride out the volatile returns of stocks over long periods of time are generally rewarded with strong, positive returns.

Bonds are generally less volatile than stocks, but offer more modest returns. As a result, an investor approaching a financial goal might increase his or her bond holdings relative to his or her stock holdings. The reduced risk of holding more bonds would be attractive to the investor, despite their lower potential for growth, because the goal is within reach. You should keep in mind that certain categories of bonds offer high returns similar to stocks. These bonds, known as high-yield or junk bonds, also carry a higher risk, too.

Cash and cash equivalents—such as savings deposits, certificates of deposit, Treasury bills, money market deposit accounts, and money market funds—are the safest investments, but offer the lowest return of the three key asset categories. The chances of losing money on an investment in this asset category are generally extremely low. The federal government guarantees many investments in cash equivalents. Investment losses in nonguaranteed cash equivalents do occur, but infrequently. The principal concern for investors investing in cash equivalents is inflation risk. This is the risk that inflation will outpace and erode investment returns over time.

Stocks, bonds, and cash are the most common asset categories and they are the ones you would likely choose from when investing in a retirement savings program. But other asset categories—including real estate, precious metals and other commodities, and private equity—also exist, and some investors may include these asset categories within a portfolio. Investments in these asset categories typically have category-specific risks.

Historically, the returns of the three major asset categories have never moved up and down at the same time. By including asset categories with investment returns that move up and down under different market conditions within a portfolio, an investor can protect against significant losses. Market conditions that cause one asset category to do well often cause another asset category to have average or poor returns. By investing in more than one asset category, you'll reduce the risk that you'll lose money and your portfolio's overall investment returns will have a smoother ride. If one asset category's investment return falls, you will be in a position to counteract your losses in that asset category with better investment returns in another asset category.

CHAPTER EIGHT

The Importance of Rebalancing

"The Chinese use two brush strokes to write the word 'crisis.' One brush stroke stands for danger; the other for opportunity. In a crisis, be aware of the danger—but recognize the opportunity."
—John F. Kennedy

To the average observer, the physics of a balanced cargo load may seem insignificant, but people in the shipping industry know how important it is. Big shippers spend millions each year perfecting the science of properly positioning cargo on their planes, ships, and trucks. If loaded properly, the transport vehicle, whatever it happens to be, will operate at peak efficiency, while an unevenly distributed load can spell disaster.

Balance is just as vital in our portfolios. And since the market is susceptible to shifts and changes, it is necessary to look at how we position our "load" on a regular basis and rebalance our holdings when necessary. Most financial professionals agree with that statement...but not necessarily how to go about it. Once again, when the opinions are extreme and polarized, I usually find that the truth is in the middle. The truth here is that there is no set formula. There is no one-size-fits-all solution. The truth is that how we arrange asset classes within a portfolio (call it the *mix*) varies significantly according to how we view risk and what our investment goals are. The mix will be as individual as our DNA.

Over the years, I have sat with thousands of clients and conducted extensive interviews to ascertain their view of risk, time horizon, need for income, and overall health. I can assure you that when you plug in all those variables, every situation is different. There is no cookie-cutter formula. But once we have decided the foundational layout of the portfolio, the next objective is to make sure our portfolio doesn't drift away, taken downstream or upstream by market forces. Just as we would adjust the sound on a stereo system, or adjust the color on a television screen, adjustments made in our portfolio will be based somewhat on our comfort level. That having been said, however, it is wise to avoid letting our emotions get in the way of making sound investment decisions. Once we make the major adjustments (that is to say, once we have decided how much money will be at risk and how much will be safe and how much of each asset class we will employ) then the minor adjustments can be made as the market dictates. I like to call this "tweaking" the portfolio.

Tweaking by the Numbers

A word of caution: if we tweak by the numbers, or according to the disciplines we have already set for our investing, some of these adjustments may be counterintuitive. They may not feel right to us at the time we make them. But if we are not to make the buy-high–sell-low mistake, we have to learn to sell out of a position when it is on its run up. When it reaches its target, we follow our advisor's recommendation to pull the sell trigger, even if we are thinking to ourselves, "The run isn't over...there's more to be made in this stock or sector." The same would be true of stocks or sectors that have lost ground and are nearing their bottom. No, we don't know what an individual stock will do on a given day, but sectors and asset classes are predictable *to a point*, and they generally behave truer to the pattern.

Let's say, for example, that equity markets are having a good run, and we want to accept a bit more risk to take advantage of it. We may wish to "tweak" our portfolio from, let's say, a 60% stocks and 40% bonds mix to a 70% stocks and 30% bonds mix. If, however, the numbers dictate that it would be wise to retreat a bit, then we may rebalance our portfolio to its original position. To illustrate why emotion can be the barrier to rebalancing, just look at a historical performance of asset-classes from 1997 through 1999. This was a period when, if it were a foot race, US growth stocks left US value stocks and international stocks in the dust, while bonds gasped for air and crossed the finish line dead last.

Many investors wanted to let these winners continue to run. "If they won the last heat, they will win the others," they reasoned. Their portfolios had become heavy with growth stocks, which they considered "winners," and that's all they could see. Not only did many investors leave their portfolios overweight in these growth stock speedsters, they even *added* to their growth stock allocations. I call that "chasing returns." By early 2000, growth stocks had run their course for the next two years and they trailed all other asset classes. Bonds, however, had caught a second wind and had moved from worst to first. That's why I call rebalancing a discipline. There are selling and buying trigger points that a competent investment coach will be able to identify for you using a formulaic approach, not his gut feelings. Staying with those trigger points is a rational, measured way to control the risks in your portfolio and come out the winner.

Rebalancing can also be done by simply adding more money to our portfolio. It may be prudent to invest more into fixed income vehicles by withdrawing money from equities and reinvesting the proceeds into fixed income to bring the mix back to a safer position.

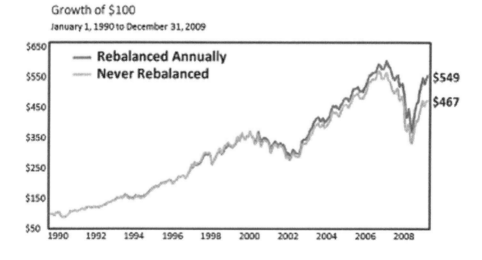

Growth of $100
January 1, 1990 to December 31, 2009

Some advisors like to rebalance on a fixed schedule, just like one might change the oil in an automobile every three to four thousand miles. I suppose that is better than not doing maintenance at all. But I believe that because financial markets are inherently unpredictable, you should realign your portfolio as changes within the market create imbalances. Call it "real-time rebalancing" if you want. Use the example of a truck driver hauling a flatbed load of building materials. The driver would certainly check the distribution of his load at regular intervals, such as fuel stops. But after rounding a sharp curve and feeling the natural forces of gravity and centrifugal force at work on his load, he would most certainly stop to make sure the load was still properly distributed.

So it is with our portfolio. We cannot predict when there will be a shift in the market that could cause our portfolio to drift out of balance. But to ignore such a shift when it occurs, just because it wasn't on our rebalancing schedule, is faulty reasoning. We shouldn't wait until a calendar says it's time to tweak. What if it was *your* portfolio in early 2000 and your growth stock exposure had grown too large? What would have happened if you had waited until the end of the year to rebalance? A critical risk exposure would have been ignored.

A disciplined rebalancing process prompts investors to act when changes in the portfolio require action. As an added benefit, when markets are stable, and the portfolio is reasonably close to its target allocations, it won't prompt them to do anything.

Rebalancing forces you to remember why you came to the table. It keeps you on task with your allocation targets. Just like guardrails keep you on the road and away from the cliff, rebalancing keeps you within your preset risk-tolerance boundaries. Your decisions at the beginning had to do with your broad picture.

You chose your risk tolerance and your time horizon carefully. The last thing you want to do is to allow the movements of the market to play havoc with those presets. You will be prudent to make changes only when they are in harmony with your long-term financial planning. If you are like most people, every year that ticks by should signal you to get a little more conservative with your investing than you were the previous year. Typically, the older you are, the less money you will have in stocks.

When to Rebalance: The Trigger Point

Each asset class is unique. Each will have its own trigger point based on the rebalancing benefits weighed against the rebalancing costs. Some assets may have low volatility but high trading costs, while others may bear more risk but have a high correlation to other assets in the portfolio. It is the interaction among all of these factors that determines the trigger point. Your investment coach will be able to help you set those trigger points so that they make sense, both to you and for your portfolio.

CHAPTER NINE

Finally—The Truth About Annuities

"..More myths circle this investment than almost any other investment I know about. In some cases, annuities make sense, and in others they do not."

—Suze Orman

Name something controversial in the medical field. It could be anything…a controversial surgical procedure…a controversial new drug…a controversial discovery. And you will find such a dichotomy among these professionals that it makes you wonder how they could all be in the same line of work.

In the financial world, it's that way with annuities. Some swear at them, and some swear by them. And there seems to be no middle ground on the subject. One magazine article fires a salvo condemning annuities, claiming that they "lock up your money" for too long a period of time. Then another article fires right back, pointing out how reasonable the free withdrawal provisions are. Experts on one side of the table will fume over surrender charges while colleagues on the other side cry "foul" and defend them as a fair trade-off for safety and a guaranteed income stream.

As is so often the case, the truth is in the middle. Annuities had a makeover in the decade of the 2000s, and they deserve a second look, especially by retirees who want to explore all their options for retirement. Are annuities right for everyone? No. Should they be part of a retiree's portfolio? It depends, of course, on the individual's age, goals, and a number of other suitability factors.

Just as continuing education is important to the medical profession, competent financial counselors seek to keep their finger on the pulse of their profession by constantly doing the two Rs—reading and research. Prescribing the wrong medicine can affect the patient's health. Recommending a financial strategy in error can affect the client's wealth.

I have heard of horror stories to the contrary, but I would like to think that it would be rare indeed for a medical professional to allow money to affect his or her thinking when it came to medical advice. So it should be with financial professionals. If you follow the money trail, you may see why there is such a divergence of views on annuities. In my opinion, it is always best to deal with a Registered Investment Advisory firm, which has a fiduciary relationship with their clients.

We do not use the word *fiduciary* often in everyday conversation, but it is an interesting word. It comes from Latin *fiduciarius*, which means "holding in trust." A cousin word, one that has the same root, to fiduciary is *fidelity*, which has to do with truth and trust.

Fiduciary is also a legal term. Certain agents are sworn to be a fiduciary when handling another's financial affairs. Legally, fiduciaries are expected to be faultlessly loyal to persons with whom they do business. Legal fiduciaries are obligated by covenant not to put their own personal interests before the one to whom they owe this loyalty. While they may profit from the transaction, they must not profit from their position of trust.

Active money managers, who deal in stocks and bonds and whose education, certification, and affiliations dictate that their practice has to be limited to equities and stock market trading, will probably not be eager to become knowledgeable about insurance products, which they usually cannot offer. When they do their research on annuities, it may be with a jaundiced eye, looking only for the negative aspects.

By the same token, insurance agents, whose education, certification, and affiliations limit them to offering only retirement products provided by the insurance industry, are not likely to make themselves students of the stock market. When they do their research on equities, they are not likely to look at them open-mindedly as a means by which one can prosper, but will focus only on the risk that they involve. This, I believe, accounts for the opposing dialogue exchanged by these two camps. It reminds me of soldiers in the Civil War. They would often meet up with each other during truces and swap food and tobacco and even newspapers. They spoke the same language. But the next day, they would go back to shooting at each other.

So, as I said, the truth is usually always somewhere in the middle. A financial advisor who has both equity strategies and insurance strategies to offer, and one who has a fiduciary responsibility (a registered investment advisory firm) to clients will be inclined to see both sides of the picture and offer balanced and reasonable opinions.

Statistics: Annuities on the Rise

One strong indication that annuities cannot be all bad is the fact that there are so many of them out there. The Life Insurance and Market Research Association, which is better known by its acronym, LIMRA, reported that annuity sales reached $240.3 billion in 2011, an 8% increase over the previous year.[8]

Some of the more vitriolic pieces I have read on the subject of fixed and fixed indexed annuities seem to have been written by brokers, or published in magazines in which brokers advertise. From my perch, they seem to have a vested interest in keeping the public away from programs from which they cannot profit. Frankly, the more extreme their views, the more their motives seem suspect. If millions of Americans are buying annuities, it may be unwise to call all of them "stupid."

Does volume equal validity? Not always; but in this case, it makes a pretty strong point. Did you notice in the chart shown here that when the stock market disappoints, annuities become more popular? Did you also notice that when the market is doing well, annuity sales are lower? There is a reason for this. Fixed and fixed indexed annuities, while some of them may reflect the upside of the market in their returns, are contractually immune from the losses of the market. Investors seeking ultimate safety, then, will tend to gravitate toward these insurance products in times of market instability. Since those approaching retirement and those already in retirement are the most concerned about safety and income, it stands to reason

---

8   Stanley, Michael K. "LIMRA Reports on Annuity Sales." March 6, 2012. http://www.lifehealthpro.com/2012/03/16/limra-reports-on-annuity-sales.

that they are the largest target audience for fixed and fixed indexed annuities.

Don't Throw the Baby Out With the Bathwater!

Before we lump all annuities together, let's establish that they are not all created equal. The starting place is to know the difference between the *fixed* annuity and the *variable* annuity.

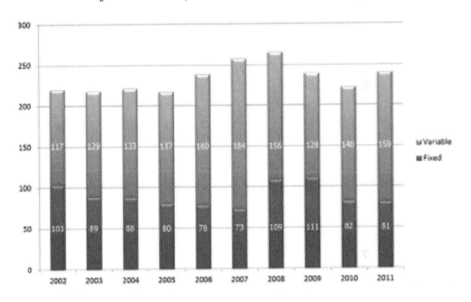

Fixed Annuities

A fixed annuity is a contract offered by an insurance company that is much like a bank certificate of deposit. Just like a CD, you deposit a certain amount of money and the insurer agrees to pay a certain interest rate over a specified period of time. That's basically it. But a couple of things make a fixed annuity slightly different. On the plus side, unlike with a bank CD, the interest you earn in a fixed annuity isn't taxed until you withdraw the money. If you withdraw those fixed-annuity interest earnings before age fifty-nine and a half, however, you will not only pay income tax, but a 10% penalty.

In addition, insurers typically charge an early withdrawal penalty for withdrawals made within the first five to ten years that you own the annuity. These early withdrawal penalties can start as high as 10% or so (even higher in some cases) and then usually decline by a percentage point or so until they disappear after five to ten years. There is a subcategory under fixed annuities that has been called a *hybrid* annuity. The insurance industry, which developed it around 2004 or so, calls it *a fixed indexed annuity*. It combines the safety of the fixed annuity with the capacity to earn a portion of the returns that track the growth (but not the downside) of the stock market.

Variable Annuities

A variable annuity works somewhat like a mutual fund. You invest in one or more subaccounts, which can own stocks or bonds or a combination of stocks and bonds. With fixed indexed annuities, you are not actually *in the market*. Your returns are merely predicated on an index which reflects the market. With a variable annuity, you *are* actually in the market. You have a possibility of greater returns along with the possibility of loss.

So what's the difference between a retail mutual fund and a variable annuity? For one, a variable annuity has an extra set of fees, usually known as insurance costs or mortality and expense (M&E) charges. These fees, while they are paying for a greater measure of protection from risk, give variable annuities higher annual operating expenses than mutual funds. Between the normal management fees required to run the underlying investments and the insurance charges, the fees associated with a VA can be 3% or more. Fixed annuities do not have these fees.

As with a fixed annuity, any earnings in a variable annuity remain untaxed as long as they remain in the annuity. When you draw them out, they are taxed as ordinary income, just like a fixed annuity.

Risk versus Return

There is a risk versus return trade-off with variable and fixed annuities. The fixed annuity provides more security of principal than a variable annuity but can have less upside potential. You accept more short-term volatility when you invest in a variable annuity. You can see the value of your investment fluctuate with the stock market with a variable annuity, whereas the fixed annuity is contractually guaranteed never to retreat in value unless you reach in and take the money out.

Fixed Indexed Annuities

According to the LIMRA report, 2011 saw a marked increase in the sale of fixed indexed annuities, which captured 44% of the fixed annuity market overall. Why are they so popular lately? Several reasons:

- Retiring baby boomers seeking safety
- New lifetime income riders

- Death benefit riders for wealth transfer
- Health-care riders for long-term care
- Returns linked to stock market index
- Market downturn of 2008 raised consciousness regarding risk

Each company can have a number of choices you can utilize to calculate your return on a year-by-year basis. But unlike variable annuities, you will be able to lock in your gains on an annual basis. I always recommend a balanced approach when creating an income plan. A combination of managed money to combat inflation with some guaranteed cash flow to provide these essential expenses needed to maintain your desired lifestyle.

With regard to the fixed indexed annuity, it needs to be made abundantly clear that while they earn returns based on a stock market index, like the S&P 500, they are more of a savings vehicle than they are an investment vehicle. This product is meant to protect your principal and lock in your gains as they accrue, as well as to be a vehicle to generate guaranteed income. Over time, it should produce a better return than a standard fixed annuity. Because an indexed annuity captures only a portion of market returns, money invested directly in the market has the ability to out-produce the indexed annuity. It stands to reason that when you eliminate any risk of loss, you are by default expecting less in the way of a return. That's the trade-off. You have the peace of mind that comes with safety of principal. You know that if 2008 happens again, you won't lose 30–50% of your principal in any given year. But when the market soars on the rebound, you can't expect to participate fully in that joyous event, either.

Your contract cap, which varies each year according to the current economic climate, is a ceiling for gains just as the lock-in provision is a floor for losses.

I still have complete belief in the market long term for a portion of your money. But it should be noted that you need a minimum of ten years as the hold period. Some may even ratchet that up to fifteen to twenty years, given the extreme volatility we have experienced the last few years, not to mention the major economic challenges we are currently facing: $16 trillion in national debt, $1.3 trillion budget deficit, unemployment, the real estate crisis, Greece, Spain, Portugal, etc. At the very least most of us need to rethink this whole issue of time horizon on our at-risk portfolios. See the graph below to examine the range of expected returns based on a look back over the last twenty years.

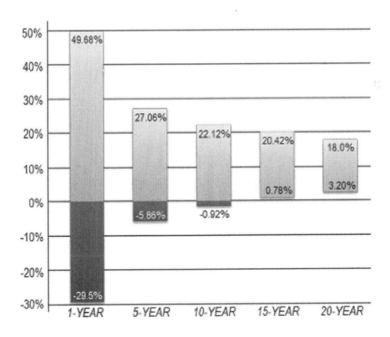

As you can see, not even ten years is a guaranteed positive return. The lost decade of 2000–2009 is still in everybody's mind.

CHAPTER TEN

The Truth About Life Insurance

"Life insurance is really weird. You really don't get anything for it. You pay me money. And when you die, I'll pay you money."

—Teenager defining life insurance

There are some things we just love owning. Our cars, for instance, we adore them and dote over them. If space aliens were to descend on our planet on a warm Saturday afternoon, they would conclude that automobiles were the dominant species on the earth, given the way their owners groom and pamper them.

Other things, however, we own because we have to, or at least feel like we do. Life insurance falls into that category. It's one of those things that most responsible people own, even though they probably resent having to pay for it.

Of all the financial planning tools available to us, life insurance is possibly the most misunderstood and undervalued. This is mainly due to the perception that most people have of life insurance, that all it does is provide a death benefit to a beneficiary in the event of the policy holder's death. One dictionary defined life insurance as "a policy people buy to protect them in case a breadwinner dies." Of course, that is essentially true. But such a simple definition of such a multifaceted financial tool is a little like calling a computer a paperless typewriter. There is just so much more to it than that.

Uses for Life Insurance

Life insurance has several unique advantages that can be used in financial planning, which is why I like to consider it as an asset class in your portfolio.

Replace Lost Income—Let's say that a couple depends upon two Social Security checks and a pension to pay necessary expenses. If one dies, a life insurance policy fills that financial void.

Protection Against Catastrophic Injury, Illness—Some insurance companies have made dramatic changes to their contracts in the last ten years, adding additional benefits such as asset-based long-term care (LTC). It is basically a single premium life insurance policy with a long-term care rider attached to it. This can be a good solution as it overcomes the objection many people have of paying for LTC that they may not use, as well as protecting against LTC insurance premium rates increasing. For example, you can fund the insurance policy with a $50,000 lump sum. The funds are guaranteed by the insurance company and you can get your money back at any time. Any benefits paid would, of course, lower that dollar amount. Let's use some ball-park numbers for a sixty-two-year-old female to illustrate. The $50,000 would give her approximately $90,000 in death benefit on day one, and provides about $200,000-$250,000 in long-term-care benefits. She has effectively quadrupled her money for long-term-care purposes. If she doesn't end up needing the care, the death benefit can be passed on to her heirs. Funds earning little or nothing in savings or a CD can be redirected to provide long-term-care, meaning she has transferred the risk of self-funding for long-term-care. Other provisions allow the policy holder to use a portion of the death benefit in the event of a critical illness, such as heart attack, stroke, or cancer.

Facilitate Transfer of Wealth to Heirs—Many do not realize that Uncle Sam is their biggest beneficiary. Life insurance can be used strategically to avoid unnecessary taxation. By law, the proceeds from a life insurance policy are generally free from federal income taxes. It is possible to buy a life insurance policy inside an irrevocable life insurance trust (ILIT) and thereby avoid estate taxes. A properly created ILIT is the owner and the beneficiary of the policy. Because you do not own the life insurance—the ILIT does—the life insurance proceeds are not subject to federal estate tax. One of the characteristics of a properly structured ILIT is that it is irrevocable, meaning you can't change it once you've set it up. But that feature lets you control who gets the life insurance proceeds. Why is that significant? Can you think of a situation where keeping the money within the possession of your blood relatives may be jeopardized by lawsuits or divorce? We live in a litigious society. This is a biggie.

Create a Private Pension—Not many know about this one. Cash value in whole life policies has been around a long time, but the traditional growth rate of the cash value within life insurance policies remained in the low single digits until a decade or so ago, when insurance companies began linking cash value growth to the performance of a stock market index, such as the S&P 500. The tax codes limit how much you can pay into a life insurance policy before it loses its tax-favored status. Some who are risk averse like the idea of paying as much as the IRS allows into a life policy, let the cash value grow tax free, then withdraw nontaxable dollars to fund retirement after enough time has passed for the compounding effect of the policy to produce what amounts to a self-made pension. This idea is made even more attractive by the lower mortality costs now enjoyed by policy holders. Insurance as an investment is not for everyone, but if you pay more than thirty cents on the dollar in taxes (see history of tax rates on next page), you may find it attractive. When weighted against a taxable investment that has downside risk, the projections are attractive. The index universal life (IUL) concept is to mirror what the market does during the upticks, up to a generous double-digit cap, then freeze in place when the downticks occur. So there is no market risk, only market-like rewards. No penalties are imposed for withdrawals before age fifty-nine and a half and there are no mandatory withdrawals after age seventy and a half.

Keep Assets Away from Creditors—State laws vary, so it is difficult to cite chapter and verse on every state, but suffice it to say that in general, the proceeds of a life insurance policy are sheltered from the grubby hands of those who might prey on the legacy you leave behind. In my home state, the Michigan Compiled Laws Annotated (MCLA) 500.2207 reads in part: *"Under Michigan law the proceeds (including cash value) of life insurance payable to spouse or children, or for their benefit, are exempt from claims of insured's creditors whether beneficiary was named originally or later by beneficiary change or assignment."*

Life Insurance as an Asset Class

As I have said before in this book, any view that is so extreme that it leaves no room for discussion is probably invalid because of its own polarization. It could be that some who deride the idea of regarding life insurance as an asset class simply do not understand all that it can do. It is just one more tool in the toolbox that, depending on the situation, can serve a useful function, particularly in income and estate planning. Every competent financial planner will know how it works, and whether it is a fit. The concept of life insurance as an asset class is a relatively new approach to helping people protect and value their lives appropriately. Life insurance can be complex. There are as many different kinds of insurance policies as there are companies that offer them, and those seem to be myriad.

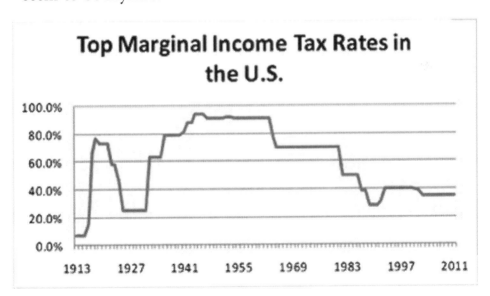

What makes life insurance a viable instrument for retirement income in many situations is its tax advantages. No other financial product that I am acquainted with enjoys quite the unique status that life insurance does. Consider the following:

- You pay no current income tax on interest or other earnings credited to cash value. As the cash value accumulates, it is not subject to current taxation.
- You pay no income tax if you borrow cash value from the policy through loans. Generally, loans are treated as debts, not taxable distributions. You are essentially borrowing your own money, so the loans need not be repaid. Compounding builds up a sizable amount of cash value in overfunded policies and this can be "borrowed" systematically to supplement a retirement income.
- Your heirs pay no income tax on the proceeds. If the death benefit is $500,000, then that's what your heirs receive: no deductions or withholding required.
- You can avoid potential estate taxes and probate costs on policy proceeds as long as the beneficiary designations and policy ownership are arranged in accordance with current law.
- As you look back at the history of tax rates (previous page) the likelihood of higher rates seem pretty certain. This will further increase the value of this tax-advantaged vehicle.

CHAPTER ELEVEN

How to Create Your Own Pension Plan

"The question isn't at what age I want to retire…it's at what income."
– George Foreman

The idea of having a regular, dependable, predictable, guaranteed income that you can't outlive is appealing to most baby boomers. Sound like a pension? Sure it does. But with pensions going the way of the wooly mammoth, most baby boomers will have to find a way to create their own pensions.

Insurance companies must have been reading the mind of the baby boom generation when they came up with *the lifetime income rider*. Members of the National Association for Fixed Annuities (NAFA) report that more than 50% of people who purchase fixed deferred annuities also choose to add an income rider. These income riders are also known as guaranteed lifetime withdrawal benefits (GLWB) or guaranteed lifetime income benefits (GLIB).

The first income riders were introduced on variable annuity products in 2003, and became available on fixed and fixed indexed annuity products two years later. Income riders provide consumers with a guaranteed income for life (similar to what annuitization provides), but without having to give up access to remaining principal—a feature that caused many consumers to shy away from annuities in the first place. By purchasing an income rider on a fixed rather than a variable annuity, the consumer benefits from the income rider while also being protected from investment risk.

The income rider is an attachment to the annuity contract. It is not free, but its cost is negligible, normally around 1%, and is subtracted from the gains, if any. It is important to note that when an income rider is attached to a fixed indexed annuity, you will pay the small rider charge out of the principal, if there are no gains.

With these new hybrid annuities, the balance of the accumulation account is paid to the annuitant's heirs upon his or her death. This is true even if the income has been started. Most contracts have liquidity features built into them, which will allow for withdrawals without penalty of up to 10% annually, and for certain emergencies.

How the Income Riders Work

In order to provide this feature, the insurance companies have to work with a formula. The payout amount for income riders is determined by a factor based on (a) the annuitant's age and (b) the income account value.

To understand it, picture a motorcycle with a sidecar. The income rider is the sidecar. Just as you can have a motorcycle without a sidecar, you can have an annuity without an income rider. But it does not work the other way around. You cannot have a standalone income rider. In the contract, you will typically see the following terms: *income account value* and *account value*. They are not the same. The income account is used for one purpose - to calculate income. The income account is a virtual account that will be credited interest at a rate set by the insurance company at the time of purchase. It is a *virtual* account while it is growing. It turns into *real money* when you trigger your lifetime income. Then it becomes like a pension that continues paying out according to the payout formula for the rest of your life. Some annuity carriers even provide for the income to increase substantially if the annuity owner has a long-term-care event (generally defined as not being able to perform two of the six activities of daily living, or ADLs), further sheltering the annuity owner's other assets. The concern here is that one spouse could impoverish the other with a prolonged long-term-care event. In addition, the annuity owner retains access to the annuity's remaining value and continues to reap the benefits of interest credits to the annuity's value.

The income account usually has a crediting method applied to it by the insurance company. Typically, It will grow by anywhere from 4% to 8%; *that is, as long as the income is not taken.* Once the income is triggered, the growth in these accounts typically stops.

The payout formula can vary from one carrier to another, but the longer you wait to turn on your income stream, the more income you will have, for two reasons. (1) You are older, and the formula pays out a greater percentage, (2) Your account has accrued more interest. Like a garden, let the income account grow until it reaches its target growth, and the income will be higher. This can also work as an effective inflation hedge; if you have two annuities, you can draw from one account while the other continues to accumulate.

Annuitization Is Not Always a Bad Thing

When creating an income stream with an income rider, you are not annuitizing an annuity. You are merely exercising an option provided by the rider. When an annuity is annuitized, the client opts to receive payments for a designated period of time, perhaps even for life. But there is a trade-off. The annuitant swaps control of the principal for a guaranteed lifetime payout, usually at a higher rate than you could get with an income rider or even long term corporate bonds.

Annuitization is not always a bad thing, as some would have you believe. I once had an eighty-four-year-old client who was accustomed to receiving $1,000 per month in income. Then her husband died. The pension did not include a survivor option. She had $100,000, sitting in a CD earning about 1% per year in interest. That works out to be about $80 per month in income. If she began taking the $920 per month from her principal to make up for the deficit, that would make her whole for a few years. But her mother had lived into her late nineties, and my client worried that she might run out of money if she were blessed with the same longevity. So she purchased a single premium immediate annuity (SPIA) with the $100,000, and annuitized. The life option yielded her 13.4% annually or a little more than $1,100 per month for as long as she lives. In effect, *she transferred the risk of living too long to the insurance company.* This was a good move for the entire family. The woman's daughter is free from the worry that she will eventually have to bear the expense of caring for her aging mother. The mother is relieved from the fear of having to swallow her pride by asking for help to make ends meet. She can now enjoy a few of life's extras, such as eating out and buying gifts for the grandchildren. Gone are the worries about running out of money. Yes, even the dreaded SPIA (single premium immediate annuity) has its place sometimes.

Making the Case for Annuities

The Government Accountability Office (GAO) is an investigative arm of Congress charged with examining matters relating to the receipt and payment of public funds. In a July 2011 report, the GAO came out with this bit of advice for seniors facing a money shortage in retirement: Delay taking Social Security and buy an annuity.[9]

"The risk that retirees will outlive their assets is a growing challenge," the GAO points out, adding that while high-income households generally don't need them, middle- income households that don't have traditional pensions should consider using a portion of their savings to purchase an inflation-adjusted annuity.

So why is the GAO pushing annuities? Because, as the study points out, almost half of those nearing retirement are predicted to

---

9 Collins, Margaret. "Delay Taking Social Security, Add Annuity to Survive Retirement, GAO Says." *Bloomberg.com.* July 1, 2011. http://www. bloomberg.com/news/2011-07-01/delay-social-security-add-annuity-to-outlive-savings-gao-says.html.

run out of money and will not be able to cover their basic expenses and uninsured health-care costs. An immediate annuity can protect retirees from the risk of outliving their savings, according to the study. For example, a contract purchased for $95,500 by a sixty-six-year-old couple in Florida may provide $4,262 a year until the death of the surviving spouse and include increases for inflation, the report said. The GAO also recommended that retirees wait until at least full retirement age, or age sixty-six for those born from 1943 to 1954, to start taking Social Security. While the Social Security program allows recipients to take reduced payments as early as age sixty-two, it provides full benefits at age sixty-six and increases payouts by at least 32% for those who wait up to age seventy.

Jim Cramer Says What??

Jim Cramer is known for his antics on the *Mad Money* segment of television's CNBC channel. Cramer is a self-appointed guru on the stock market. On pages 67 and 68 of his book *Real Money— Sane Investing in an Insane World*[10], he says the following:

> *Your fifties begins the big shift toward more and more fixed income. And finally in your sixties, unless, again, you keep working, fixed income should dominate. Your opportunities to grow your money are now limited and the reward isn't worth the risk.*
>
> *Others in their sixties want my blessing to keep the vast majority of their assets in stocks. But I never bend on this. Here's why. I recognize the vulnerability of equities and the*

---

10   Cramer, Jim. *Jim Cramer's Real Money: Sane Investing in an Insane World.* New York: Simon & Schuster, 2005.

fallibility of my own judgment. Let's wind the tape back for a second to the spring of 2000. While I sensed that equities were overvalued, had I blessed a nontraditional nonprudent course of action—staying in equities, particularly the kind of equities people were drawn to in that era—I could have wiped out people if they overstayed their equity exposure. You never know when it is going to be the spring of 2000 again, and you can't allow your judgment to be swayed by the chance to make more money in stocks than they might allow.

Only as you get closer to needing the money should your caution take hold so that you don't let a lifetime's worth of savings be wiped out by a swift downturn in the market right before you need the money. People who want to speculate in their retirement streams, particularly when they are older, will not get my blessing.

My interpretation regarding Cramer's remarks is not to risk money needed to fund your essential expenses. Once you have these expenses covered it allows you to take some measured risk with your discretionary funds.

Wharton Report

Remember the old E. F. Hutton commercials of the 1970s and 1980s? Two young professionals are talking in a crowded room and one mentions the name, E. F. Hutton, and suddenly the room falls silent, everyone leaning in to get an earful of some profound statement from the founder of the brokerage firm by the same name. Then the throaty voice would intone: "When

E. F. Hutton talks…people listen." The firm named after Mr. Hutton was apparently lost in the shuffle of several mergers in the 1980s, but the commercial catchphrase lingers. In my opinion, the Wharton Financial Institutions Center has that sort of prestige today, particularly in the area of personal finance. As one economics expert put it, "If their researchers were working on cancer, we would already have a cure."

Professors Craig B. Merrill and Professor David F. Babbel, leading academics in retirement income planning, recently produced an independent research paper which had the following comment about annuities: "In the case of life annuities, the risk of outliving one's income is pooled among all annuity purchases, providing a kind of insurance against outliving one's assets." They went on to say that a life annuity is "the only investment vehicle that allows its owners an income to spend at the same rate, but be covered for as long as they live."[11] To my knowledge, neither Professor Merrill nor Professor Babbel sells annuities.

A 2010 Wharton Report entitled, *Real World Index Annuity Returns,* compared the returns of indexed annuities with those of the stock market.[12] This favorable comment was made on page nine of the report: "for moderate and strongly risk-averse

11   Babbel, David F., and Craig B. Merrill. "Investing Your Lump Sum at Retirement." Wharton Financial Institutions Center. August 14, 2007. Http://fic.wharton.upenn.edu/fic/policy%20page/whartonessay18.pdf.
12   Marrion, Jack, Geoffrey VanderPal, and David F. Babbel. "Real World Index Annuity Returns." Wharton Financial Institutions Center. October 5, 2009. http://annuitythinktank.com/Portals/0/Documents/wharton%20white%20paper.pdf.

individuals, the fixed indexed annuity is judged superior in performance to various combinations of stocks and bonds."

What is a Safe Withdrawal Rate?

Retirement planning academics analyzed historical returns of stocks and bonds and found the 4% withdrawal rate rule could put you in danger of running out of money.[13] They found that portfolios with 60% of their holdings in large cap stocks and 40% in intermediate-term US bonds sustained withdrawal rates starting at 4.15% adjusted each year for inflation, for every thirty year span dating back to 1926-1955. The problem is if you lose 25% of your portfolio at the beginning of your payment stream. To quote *Wall Street Journal's* "Saying Goodbye to the 4% Rule:"

> *"If you had retired Jan. 1, 2000, with an initial 4% withdrawal rate and a portfolio of 55% stocks and 45% bonds rebalanced each month, with the first year's withdrawal amount increased by 3% a year for inflation, your portfolio would have fallen by a third through 2010, according to investment firm T. Rowe Price Group. And you would be left with only a 29% chance of making it through three decades"*

For most baby boomers, the thought of running out of money is one of their predominant fears regarding retirement.

---

13 Greene, Kelly. "Say Goodbye to the 4% Rule." *Wall Street Journal.* 1 Mar. 2013. <http://online.wsj.com/article/SB10001424127887324162304578304491492559684.html>.

In the same article, Professor Pfau of the American College of Financial Services says "There is no need for retirees to hold bonds. Instead, annuities, with their promise of income for life, act like super bonds with no maturity dates."

An annuity can eliminate the chance of running out of money on a portion of your portfolio by eliminating interest rate risk, market volatility, credit risk, etc., inherent with individual securities. Think of an annuity as being synonymous with a pension. By creating a second or a third pension you will be adding to your foundational income and hopefully your peace of mind.

Annuities have their place. They are not the be-all and end-all, but there is a place for them in a balanced portfolio, especially for retirees seeking to guarantee a portion of their income. This is particularly true for retirees who will need additional income to cover their living expenses if their pension, assuming they have one, and Social Security does not cover their essential monthly expenses.

CHAPTER TWELVE

The Red and Green Money Balancing Act

"Stop trying to predict the direction of the stock market, the economy, interest rates, or elections"

– Warren Buffett

Risk tolerance is huge when it comes to properly distributing investments. Most folks, as they move into retirement, aren't keen on losing money. So, for these individuals, it's important to control volatility. I will never forget one particular couple who became clients shortly before they retired. They were both bright people, educators, in fact. Our initial conference, the one where I do most of the listening and the client does most of the talking, went well. I learned much about them and what kind of lifestyle they envisioned for themselves in retirement. They both had an interest in travel but each for different reasons. She loved to gamble and enjoyed playing the penny slots at all the casinos. He, on the other hand, was an amateur golfer. His passion was the challenge of trying to master the greens of all the courses he played.

In our second meeting, when I tried to explain exactly how we could position their assets to provide them with a comfortable retirement, I could tell there was a disconnect. I wasn't getting through to them. It was then that I got the idea of illustrating what I meant with the colors of a traffic light. We began connecting after that.

Red Money—Green Money

Green money is safe money. These are the assets that come with defined rates of return. They cannot go down in value. They are generally used to produce additional income and form the bedrock of an income stream. We use green money to take care of living expenses, like rent, food, and transportation. If we have a fixed annuity, that's green money because it is safe from market risk and could provide an income stream. If we have money in CDs, that's green money. You get the idea.

Red money, on the other hand, is money that you invest at some degree of risk. You can afford this degree of risk because (a) you have identified your risk tolerance factor, and (b) you have enough green money set aside as a safety net. Red money needs at least a ten-year time horizon to be effective. With the risk comes a greater growth potential. Since we don't know exactly how this money will perform, we exercise more caution with our red money the older we get. In our rebalancing, we shift more from red money to green money as we age and approach retirement.

Subcategories may exist in these two colors of money, but that is basically it. The key component with the red money is time. The more time you have to let the system work for you, the more red money you should have. It generally conforms pretty closely to the "rule of one hundred," which states that you take one hundred and subtract your age from it. The resulting number suggests the maximum amount of risk exposure you should have in your portfolio. Example: for a person age sixty-five, the equation is: $100 - 65 = 35\%$ maximum subject-to-market risk. The rest should be green money. Before we ever launch a portfolio together, I insist on a heart-to-heart talk with clients about emotions and market timing. Good coaching, I believe, helps to dispel unwarranted fear. The most common fear is fear of the unknown. Understanding the mechanics at work within a portfolio, replaces clients' fear with knowledge and enables them to make good decisions and avoid bad ones.

You've heard the adage, "Buy low and sell high." Bad timing is when you sell out of a position or buy into one at the wrong time. No one would do this intentionally. Problem is, investors sometimes have 20/20 hindsight when it comes to implementing the buy-low–sell-high rule of thumb because of emotion. Without good coaching, what usually happens is that an investor will catch wind of something that influences his thinking. It could be news of a change in the economy in general, or a tidbit of information about a particular stock or asset class. The investor, driven by emotion, senses pressure to act on this information in the hope of making a smart move—to catch the train before it leaves the station. But more often than not, by the time he or she has that notion and acts on it, the news is already in the stock. That is, the share price of the stock already reflects whatever influence this news has had on it. If that is the case, then a move to buy the stock then is made at precisely the wrong time. And when the winds shift the other way, we compensate by acting in the opposite direction. And, once again, we are too late.

If I could build this phrase out of cinderblock letters and put neon lights around it and make the lights blink on and off, I would do it:

IT'S IMPOSSIBLE TO TIME THE MARKET.

Not too long ago, I had a client call me up who, only two months previously, had put money into a managed account. The client informed me that the account was down. I had to remind the investor about an earlier conversation, one that took place before the plan was put into action, when we had discussed the fact that a ten-to-fifteen-year hold time would be necessary for this type of investing to work. He remembered, and all was fine. But the urge to overreact is normal, and the tendency of new investors is to make too many minor course changes and lose their way.

Discipline and Patience Required

Two months after the 9/11 attack on the World Trade Center, American Airlines flight 587 crashed into the Belle Harbor neighborhood of Queens, a borough of New York City, killing all 260 aboard and five on the ground. At first, the crash was thought to have been the result of another terrorist plot. But that was ruled out after an investigation revealed that the disaster was caused by the first officer's overuse of rudder controls in response to wake turbulence from another airplane. The turbulence had caused the plane to yaw slightly. The copilot then applied too much pedal to the tail rudder. The big plane swerved too far in the opposite direction. The copilot over corrected again, and by that time the plane was out of control and crashed. Investigators with the National Transportation Safety Board said, "If the first officer had stopped making additional inputs, the aircraft would have stabilized."

Similarly, investors will sometimes see that a particular holding is losing ground, so their first reaction is to sell before it loses any more. Then, when the stock or asset class rebounds, they attempt to recover when it's too late. Like the copilot of the jet, had they done nothing at all, they would have been better off.

The independent research firm, DALBAR, claims that the biggest determinant to portfolio returns is market timing—simply getting in and out of the markets at the wrong time. According to DALBAR, a classic example is the period from 1992 through 2011 when the S&P 500 returned an average of approximately 8%. Not bad! But the average investor earned a mere 3.5% during the same period. Why were the individual investor returns so low?

- Buying and selling too often
- Not holding onto the accounts long enough.
- Chasing the market (track record investing)
- Hyperactive stock picking
- Trying to time the market

CATEGORY	1992-2011 Annualized Return
S&P 500 Index	7.81%
Average Equity Fund Investor	3.49%
Inflation	2.51%

*DALBAR, Inc., *Quantitative Analysis of Investor Behavior*, 2012
Results are based on the twenty-year period from 1992-2011

If those common investment mistakes sound familiar, you are not alone. The average holding period for individual investors is 3.11 years. That is simply not enough time. Think in terms of at least ten years or more for the system to work for you.

Using Investment Tools

I'm not much of a do-it-yourself guy. I have a few basic tools in my garage: two hammers, a handsaw, an assortment of screwdrivers, pliers, and a measuring tape or two. They come in handy from time to time if the job isn't too complicated. But I have it on good authority that you don't use the measuring tape to drive a nail into a plank. And you don't use a hammer to cut a board in half, either. That doesn't mean that the hammer is no good, or the measuring tape doesn't work. It just means that every tool has its purpose.

Likewise, every investment type has its specific purpose, depending on what your objective is. Let's say you are going into retirement with a decent pension…one that guarantees you a lifetime income. Let's say your Social Security checks will be coming in regularly, and between the two incomes you have all your living expenses met and then some. Then there is little need for additional guaranteed income, which means you should look at longer-term investments.

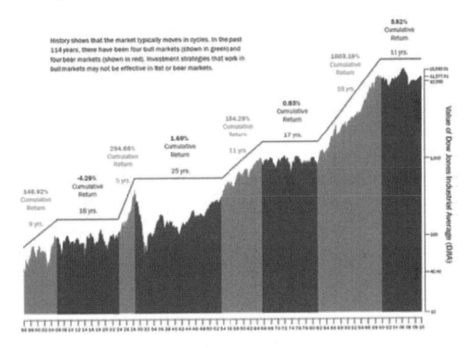

I call *green money* the "I know so" money in a portfolio, because I know that it will be there. It is not at risk. It is safe money. I know, to a point, how the investment will behave and what my returns will be. Green money is usually one of the following:

- Checking
- Savings

- Money market
- Fixed annuities
- Market linked annuities
- Market linked CDs
- TIPS (Treasury inflation protected securities)

Since this money is not at risk, the rewards of these types of investments may be limited, but that is what is needed in certain circumstances. I call *red money* the "I hope so money" in a portfolio because I don't know in the short run what the outcome of this investment will be. This is at-risk money.

- Stocks
- Bonds
- Variable annuities
- Mutual funds
- REITS (Real estate investment trusts)
- ETFs
- Options

These vehicles are meant for relatively long-term investing because we have confidence that, in the long run, you will come out ahead. Another interpretation of how to look at this is as follows: You have three categories of investments; the first two are green and the third is red. The second category of green consists of market-linked type vehicles (sometimes referred to as hybrid vehicles). Market-linked CDs, market-linked annuities, and TIPS fall into this category. They are resistant to market losses.

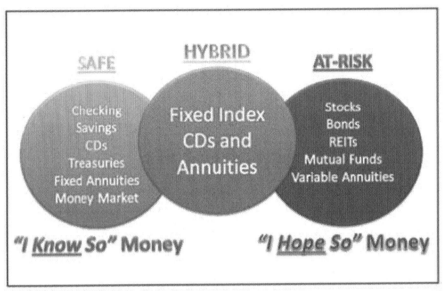

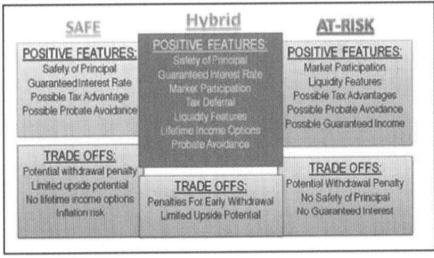

CHAPTER THIRTEEN

Building a Solid Financial Foundation

"A successful man is one who can lay a firm foundation with the bricks others have thrown at him."

—David Brinkley

When I am called upon to lecture on financial planning, I cannot resist spending at least ten minutes or so discussing the importance of starting with a good foundation. I like to tell the story of the worst natural disaster in Michigan's history—the 1953 Beecher tornado.

Michigan, the state where I live, gets its share of tornados, but it is not in what is called "tornado alley." That is farther to the southwest. But there are those who still vividly remember the Beecher tornado, and it is fascinating to hear their firsthand account of the tragic storm. It touched down the evening of June 8, 1953, in the little town of Beecher, about thirty-five miles north of my childhood town Clarkston, Michigan, my hometown. The devastating F5 twister, packing winds of around 275 miles per hour, started on the west side of town and stayed on one street, Coldwater Road, for about five miles, turning three hundred houses into splinters and killing 116 people, before capriciously lifting and heading for Lake Huron. Eyewitnesses spoke of the spectacle they witnessed when, after the disaster, they drove down Coldwater and saw all the homes gone. The only things left were foundations, sitting there, as if beckoning on behalf of the former dwelling, asking to be rebuilt. And that is the point: foundations. When those people returned to their homes to begin, quite literally, picking up the pieces of their lives, there was not much left. But from those foundations, they could start over. And they did rebuild. When you drive down that stretch of Coldwater Road today, houses sit where they always did, most of them having been rebuilt within a year after the tornado.

Creating a retirement income plan is like building a house. We begin with a stable foundation of green money investments—CDs, savings, annuities, TIPS, pensions, and Social Security—the "I know so" money previously discussed. The returns are both predictable and reliable, if not guaranteed. We know this money will be there for us when we need it. That way our fiscal house can withstand anything, even the whirlwind losses we saw in the stock market in 2008 when the market dropped by almost 50%. No matter what happens, you have a solid base. Before we do anything else, we start here. It makes no sense to decorate the walls until the foundation is in place. The formula as to how much green money needs to be used for our foundation is as straightforward as the rule of one hundred discussed earlier in this book. Again, take your age and subtract it from one hundred. That's the amount of money you should have at risk. The rest should be green money, or safe money.

With that taken care of, we can build the walls. They need to be strong and support the roof. Perhaps you remember hearing about class action lawsuits over tainted "Chinese drywall" installed in thousands of homes in Florida a few years ago. These inferior building materials were purchased by contractors because they were cheap. When homeowners began noticing a rotten-egg smell that permeated their homes and ruined their wiring, it became clear to everyone why the wallboard had been so inexpensive. It had been made from a corrosive material high in sulfur content.

When constructing our walls, we want to make them out of sturdy materials that won't crumble. Here is where we use our red money investments—stocks, bonds, mutual funds, REITS, commodities, and options. Well represented should be sturdy blue-chip companies that have been around a long time. Here, we are looking for good income and strong returns. Yes, there is a risk to principal, but these investments also have the greatest potential for gain. Remember, this is "I hope so" money, so there are no guarantees. We need to know that going in. But if we plan properly, our house will likely be capable of serving us the rest of our lives.

Last, we construct the roof. When a storm comes and brings with it hail and wind, the roof is the part of the house that usually gets most of the damage. It's the same in our financial plan. This is where we will install our high-risk, high-reward assets. Sure, they will be the first to take the hit, but at the same time they will be the first to have the biggest gain in the market. They will be the riskiest holdings you have because they are exposed to things that we cannot control that may affect the market, such as terrorist attacks, natural disasters, and a number of other things that can and do have an impact on market returns. Again, no matter what you throw at the market, given enough time—and time is definitely the key here—patience is usually rewarded with an additional return over green money type investments. Risk will be tempered, however, by proper asset allocation based on age and circumstances.

Once completed, our fiscal house should be one that will provide the appropriate amenities we will need for a lifetime in retirement.

Safety

Safety is primary. Volatility is acceptable when you are accumulating your wealth. When you are in your working years, you should always be buying more shares, even when stocks are suppressed. But when you are retired, you will be in a position of liquidating, not accumulating, shares. You are now in the distribution phase of your financial life, so safety of principal is crucial. This is no time to take chances with your money hoping to find the next Apple or Microsoft. To be clear, I still believe in equities even during the distribution phase, but it's imperative that you pay close attention as to how much you're going to allocate to stocks. We need equities in our portfolio to offset the long-term effects inflation can have on our purchasing power. As long as our house is built with a solid foundation, we should be all right.

Taxes

Being upstanding citizens, we pay our taxes. Being also of sound mind and good judgment, we want to pay only our fair share and no more. The odd thing is, we sometimes view the government as being the tyrannical ogre out to harm us, when the fact is, they provide many legitimate avenues of avoiding (notice I did not say evading) taxes, if we would but take notice of them and implement them in our financial planning. I recommend a tax review. Have your tax professional do a thorough check of your plan to make sure you are not paying more than your fair share. If you are receiving Social Security payments and you are paying taxes on them, you may not have to with proper planning. If you have a mutual fund that has gone down in value, yet you still received a 1099, it's called phantom income. The reason this occurred is because your fund manager likely sold off some gain positions in order to bolster returns, causing an increase in your "income," even though you didn't actually receive it – thus sticking you with taxes in the same year you actually incurred a loss. Because you didn't sell loss positions, gains and losses cannot be used to offset each other in this case.

Income Planning

Start by calculating how much money you will be able to count on receiving, either in the mailbox or direct deposited into your checking account when you retire. Come up with a list of those sources and the dollar figure that each will yield. Then make a notation as to how long that income stream will last.

Next, take note of whether the income is projected or guaranteed. For example, if you are receiving a Social Security check from the government of the United States of America, I will go out on a limb here and say that this will fall in the guaranteed column. Some may take issue with me on this, but, the last time I checked, the US government can print money.

If you have an annuity with an income rider, you may put that down in the guaranteed column as well. There are safeguards behind the safeguards protecting the viability of insurance policies, which is essentially what an annuity is. If the income stream is from rental property, that would probably not be guaranteed unless there is a contract with a realty company specifying continuous occupancy. Scheduled income, in the way of dividends from a brokerage account, will be projected income. If you have more projected income than you do guaranteed income, then a risk exposure evaluation may be called for. Remember, risk is not a dreadful thing, but too much of it is hazardous to your wealth in retirement. The proper mix or balance is the key factor here.

Second Opinions

We cannot imagine buying a pair of shoes two sizes too small. There is a clear reason for that. They would *hurt!* But when it comes to planning, we sometimes settle for a plan that doesn't fit our individual circumstances. We may feel uncomfortable but simply not know how to articulate that discomfort, so we go along. We do not hesitate to get a second opinion regarding a serious health issue, so I recommend that you insist on a second opinion from a financial professional if you are uncomfortable, or unsure that you are on the right path, with your current plan. In most cases, initial consultations are free. A competent professional should be able to help you take a financial snap-shot, which should enable you to understand whether or not you could be taking some additional steps to help ensure that you and your spouse are prepared for the next twenty-five to thirty years of retirement.

CHAPTER FOURTEEN

Hoping for the Best; Planning for the Worst

"First ask yourself: What is the worst that can happen?
Then prepare to accept it. Then proceed to improve on the worst."
—Dale Carnegie

In 2008, I saw a *60 Minutes* feature on dealing with uncertainty. They referred to the future, financially speaking, as "the economic maze ahead." Yes, there are some daunting pitfalls out there. Health care is one. Even if you have Medicare and the best Medicare supplement plan available, but you are one of the millions who don't have long-term care insurance, you could be in a tight spot if your health deteriorates. We hope for the best, but that doesn't mean that we don't plan for the direst of eventualities, which is why we wear seat belts and buy cars with air bags. It only makes good sense to do so. Ask your financial professional if there are programs available that will make sense for you in this area of life. With the throng of baby boomers coming to the big retirement party, insurance companies have gotten highly creative in the last few years. If you do not have long term care insurance, and you have at least $100,000 to $200,000 in underemployed assets, you may qualify for something relatively new to the marketplace that combines the characteristics of a fixed annuity with those of viable long-term-care coverage. Once you approach your sixties and seventies, cost is usually the objection to purchasing long-term-care insurance—that, and the fact that if you don't use it, you lose it. These new products, called "combos" by some in the insurance industry, don't behave that way. They may be worth a look, if your situation merits it.

It's only human nature, but we don't like to think about what will happen if we become too sick or too frail to manage our own affairs. Observers say that this attitude partly explains why sales of long-term-care insurance policies are so anemic. Only about 10% of seniors have such coverage. It's a bit of a Catch-22. Long-term-care insurance is obtainable (good health is a requirement) and affordable when folks are in their forties. That age group is also not as aware of its own mortality as those who have celebrated a few more birthdays.

Few Have Long-Term-Care Coverage

I suppose the reason that I am passionate about this issue is because I have seen so many seniors lose their savings to the sinkhole of expensive and prolonged medical care. I am convinced it is one of the main causes of wealth erosion in the country today. Have you ever noticed how much money property and casualty insurance companies pour into commercials about automobile insurance? We seldom hear so much as a whisper about LTC insurance. Just once, I would like to see a commercial featuring a little green lizard with an Australian accent talking about LTC insurance. It would work! The camera could zoom in to him sitting in an armchair, reading a book. As his face fills the screen, he could studiously remove his glasses, set his book down, and say in that cute little voice: "I'd like to talk to you about long-term-care insurance."

On second thought, it probably wouldn't work. The American public is just not interested. Youth is king, and we all want to pretend we will never get old and need such coverage. The US Department of Health and Human Services, however, says that 70% of the American population will need long-term-care services at some point after turning sixty-five. Because of the limited coverage of public programs, there is a reasonable chance you will have to pay for some or all of the services out of your personal income and savings. Even if you only need a little assistance at home with personal care, paying for it out of your pocket can wipe you out. For example, the Department of Health and Human Services National Clearing House reports that, as of 2010, you would pay more than $19,000 per year on average for a home health aide to assist three times a week.

"Many people think Medicare pays for long-term care—but it doesn't. Paying for LTC out of your personal income and resources can be very costly," said the government report. "As the demographic of our elderly population continues to change, there will be an increasing demand for long-term care. In brief, the largest increases in demand will occur for those services for which the elderly are insured the least." The baby boom generation has yet to hit this wall, but it's looming on the horizon for many, and it shows no signs of going away.

If I have learned anything over the past two decades of giving advice on money management, it is this: Every situation is different, and every issue has at least two sides. Purchasing some type of long-term-care coverage is advisable, but traditional policies are a bit complex. They have moving parts. After a waiting period, they generally pay a daily benefit for a certain number of years. They typically cover care in a nursing home, an assisted living facility, or at home. They also, depending on when you purchase them, tend to have high premiums. According to a 2009 study by Avalere Health, a research and consulting firm, a sixty-year-old might pay $200 a month for a policy that pays $150 a day for a maximum of three years. These premiums can be several thousand dollars per year as you get older. Keep in mind that you must factor in the cost of these premiums for years to come. Typically, people don't make a claim until they are in their eighties. If you do purchase a policy now, and then have to give it up in ten years because you can no longer afford to pay the premiums, nobody wins except the insurance company. Yes, premiums can be comparatively low when you are in your accumulation years. But if you are paying for college tuitions for the kids, keeping a job nailed down, paying on a home mortgage, have two cars in the garage and trying to keep the bills paid, then three decades or more can be a long time to fork out over $2,000 per year for LTC insurance. But, all things considered, if you can afford it, I encourage you to buy it before you turn sixty. If you are older than sixty, you may wish to look into one of the "combo" annuities where the advantages of long-term-care insurance and a fixed annuity are combined. Some life insurance policies now have products where a portion of the death benefit may be converted to long-term-care benefits. I encourage you to consult with a licensed insurance professional who specializes in these areas before making a decision.

LTC is Costly Care

During workshops when this topic is covered, I ask the question: "Do you think costs for long-term care will go up in the future or go down?" Invariably, the response is unanimous: "Up!" And that is the right answer. The US Department of Health and Human Services reports that, as of 2010, the median daily rate for a private room in a skilled nursing home facility was over $200 per day and rising. A semiprivate room may cost around 20% less. Inflation may cause those rates to double in the next twenty years.

What about at-home care? The average salary for a home health care professional is around $20 per hour. How about assisted living? That cost is roughly $3,200 per month, as of 2010. Even adult day care, an alternative which is growing in popularity, costs around $60 per day. The fact is, it's all very expensive. And when it comes to retirement planning, we would all rather think about traveling and relaxing on beaches with palm trees, but the truth is the truth. And the truth here is we need to consider this in our planning.

Medicare and Medicaid

Unfortunately for baby boomers, existing government programs aren't much help to the vast sea of those who would consider themselves "middle-income people." Medicare provides only limited nursing home and home-health-care coverage. Its assistance is for short-term recovery periods of less than three months. If you have been hospitalized for three days or more and then move into a Medicare-approved facility with skilled nursing care, Medicare will only pay for twenty days. You have to pick up the tab of a co-pay of $144.50 for days twenty-one to one hundred. There is no coverage after day one hundred. Medicaid, the health insurance program for low-income people, pays for about 70% of nursing home patients. But in order to qualify, people must generally have no more than a few thousand dollars in assets. The problem with many is that they are too rich to be poor and too poor to be rich.

Things You Need to Know

Some shy away from long-term-care insurance because they don't understand it. You can compare it to your auto insurance. You pay your annual premium to keep the policy in force, year after year, even if you don't need it.

Reimbursement policies are the most common. With reimbursement policies, you are reimbursed for actual charges. For example, if you buy a $200 a day policy and your bill is $150 a day, you are reimbursed $150, and the balance of the money stays in the pool. Depending on your policy, the insurer may directly pay the bill or you may have to pay first and then be paid by the insurer. If there is a remainder, that money is kept in the pool to make your benefits last longer.

The other type is an indemnity policy. In an indemnity policy, you get back all of what your policy covers. For example, if you buy a $200 a day policy and your bill is $150 a day, you still get $200 back. This is generally a more expensive type of policy than the reimbursement type.

But in either case, just like auto insurance, you file a claim when you need the services. The insurer is obligated to pay if your doctor deems you to need the care. The doctor's decision will be based on whether your physical or mental capacities are in sufficient decline that you cannot independently perform certain activities of daily living (ADLs), such as bathing, dressing, walking, etc. While you are receiving the benefits, you are typically not required to pay the premium. So the main hurdle is to determine exactly how much coverage you want and how you want the policy to pay. Just as there are deductibles with auto insurance, there are certain trade-offs you may make to lower the cost of LTC insurance—making the waiting period longer and accepting a portion of the risk yourself by lowering the daily rate. Some fine points you want to clarify will include the daily or monthly benefit amount of the coverage and what costs are in the area in which you live. The cost of care varies widely by region.

These are generalities and your insurance broker will be able to provide the specifics. When you do meet with him or her, you may wish to explore some of the new options that are available, such as hybrid policies that allow you to take up to 40% of your home healthcare benefit in cash to use any way you choose. There also inflation riders available at reasonable premiums.

Some policies have spousal provisions where the insured have access to each other's benefit pool if one needs more care than the other, or if the survivor wishes to inherit the other's unused benefits.

As with any other field of services, the insurance industry is always changing. If you have LTC coverage, you may do well to consult with an insurance professional, to make sure that you have the most recent version and to make sure that the coverage in the policy you currently have in force is adequate.

CHAPTER FIFTEEN

Playing Well in the Red Zone

"Football is like life—it requires perseverance, self-denial, hard work, sacrifice, dedication, and respect for authority."

—Vince Lombardi

Okay, you're the quarterback, and you are in what football aficionados call the "red zone," twenty yards away from the goal line. There's plenty of time on the clock, and your team needs a touchdown to win the game of retirement. Before you begin the snap count, you survey the obstacles in your path. Wall Street is incredibly volatile. Many retirees and soon-to-be retirees have seen as much as 40% of their retirement accounts disappear in the past few years. The economy remains unstable, without any real possibility of a sustained recovery anytime soon. Our nation recently hit its "debt ceiling," racking up over $16 trillion in unpaid bills.[14] The future of government-backed programs, such as Medicare and Social Security, appears more uncertain than ever before.

---

14 Sahadi, Jeanne. "U.S. hits debt ceiling." *Money.CNN.com.* May 16, 2011. http://money.cnn.com/2011/05/16/news/economy/debt_ceiling_deadline/index.htm (accessed December 7, 2011).

With that kind of snarling opposition staring you in the face, you have some decisions to make. What you cannot afford to do here is fumble. This is no time for a risky trick play that involves two pitches and a hand off. It's time for the fundamentals you know will work. "Execute properly, and you can do this," says the coach.

But what does that truly mean to you?

Well, first, it means we're facing different times and different struggles. When our parents and grandparents retired, they likely had some personal savings. They could also count on Social Security as a second leg of retirement. Finally, many of them had pensions, or guaranteed retirement incomes from their employers, that would take care of them for the rest of their lives. But with pensions no longer being offered, and Social Security on the verge of bankruptcy, you may find yourself in a position of having to blaze your own trail to retire in comfort and security.

Traditional Methods

Traditionally, retirees of other generations used two primary strategies for generating additional retirement income: The bank method and the Wall Street method. With "the bank method," they simply pulled interest off CDs. But if you cringe when you read what CD rates are, and have been for the last few years, you are not alone. You know that approach won't work in today's economic climate. Interest rates are at historic lows, generally below 2%, making it difficult on most retirees that need income.

What about the Wall Street method? In the past, with this strategy, you would simply pull 4% per year from your investments and live off that income. That may have been advisable in a less volatile market. But if you have lost money in the market, you probably can't see yourself continuing to pull the same dollar amount from an account that is at risk. That's precisely why a third approach has been developed, an approach that combines the elements of principal protection, based on the strength of the insurance industry, and the growth and inflation fighting features of structured products and managed money. The acronym SIIPS stands for structured income and inheritance planning strategy. This strategy combines the use of insurance products, including the strong new riders that provide a guaranteed retirement income and tax-favored accumulation with the power of market investments to provide pension-like incomes without risk. Let's take a closer look at SIIPS.

Think Buckets of Money

Every situation is different, so a SIIPS plan can be developed and utilized but the mix of components will vary according to the age, financial needs, and objectives of each retiree. One of the most commonly used SIIPS structures involves allocating money into "buckets" to help you systematically achieve your goals. There are two ways to solve for income. We can solve for the amount of income you will need on an annual basis and back into the amount needed to fund the plan. Or we can start with the amount of money you have available for the plan and determine how much income it will generate. Either way we do it, we tweak as we go along, adjusting the amount we use for three "time buckets" of money to generate a pension-like income for retirement, along with additional buckets geared toward growth.

BUCKET Number One—To generate income for the first five years of your plan, we place a portion of the funds into an immediate solution. It could be a series of laddered CDs that mature at different intervals to maximize the interest and still provide regular income payments. For example: While we exhaust the most liquid amount of money first for income, the rest of the money in the five-year bucket is growing at the maximum rate allowed by that particular instrument. We could use a combination of CDs and bonds, or possibly an immediate annuity. But the strategy works the same regardless of the vehicle we use and the vehicle used will depend on your unique circumstances. Once again, the goal is to provide for five years of dependable, guaranteed income.

BUCKET Number Two—The second "bucket" of money in your SIIPS plan is often referred to as the accumulation portion. Here, we look at solutions that will allow this segment to grow while those first five years of bucket number one are paying out. Starting in year six, and going through year ten, this second bucket begins paying out, providing your income for the next five-year span. All the while this is happening, the unused portion is at work, growing interest, so that the constant flow of income can continue as planned. Again, there are a number of vehicles we might use here, all based on your individual circumstances. The goal is to provide the highest income possible for this five-year period.

BUCKET Number Three – At this point, we will have successfully provided ten years of income and are now ready to begin using bucket number three, or what I call the "longevity" bucket because it has to last the rest of your life. For many, this is the most critical stage of the game, the point at which you do not wish to lose a dime in the market, and the point at which your plan must guarantee that you won't run out of money. In this "longevity" bucket, we look at products that accumulate for ten years—while your first two buckets are providing paychecks—and then, starting in year eleven, we begin drawing income from bucket number three which, because of the way it is structured, will continue paying a retirement income for as long as you live.

BUCKET Number Four—Finally we come to bucket number four. This fund will consist of risk-adjusted, managed, and structured investment vehicles providing additional liquidity and inflation protection. The income from this bucket can be started at any time, but I would recommend a hold period of fifteen years or more to account for market exposure.

Regardless of which National Football League team you pull for (I am a Lions fan, naturally) you have to admire the redzone skills of Peyton Manning, vaunted quarterback for the Indianapolis Colts until 2012, when he found a new home with the Denver Broncos. He has spent countless hours going over the playbook and watching film of the defense he is up against. All the moves he makes are calculated and choreographed. When he takes the snap and drops back to pass, he is carrying out a plan that is designed to succeed, which is why it so often does.

It is the same with us. We see the field before us, and we have the science of numbers working for us, not some ethereal gut feeling based on wishful thinking. Because life isn't football, we have the capacity of having our success at the line guaranteed, if we choose.

CHAPTER SIXTEEN

Consider Your Health to Be an Asset Class

"The poorest man would not part with health for money, but the richest would gladly part with all their money for health."
—Charles Caleb Colton

After having given the matter much thought, I have come to this conclusion: There are essentially two ways that we will produce an income when we retire. Either we will amass enough wealth so that our money, when put to work, can continue paying us not to work, or we will continue to work in our retirement years. If our course is the latter, and it seems likely for more and more members of the baby boom generation, then we may work full time for a few extra years. Or we may work part time. Or it may be a combination of the two. In the workshops I teach, working while in retirement is more and more a viable consideration. That fact requires us to consider our health to be just as much of an asset as our financial holdings.

Frankly, most of us were a bit spoiled by a stock market during the 1990s. That time produced the greatest bull market we have ever seen. Then along came what is now called "the lost decade." This is the span from 2000 to 2009, when the S&P 500 was functioning like an overloaded cargo plane on a short runway. It just could not get off the ground. The S&P 500 produced a negative return. Even if you had been in a fund that charged you nothing, you would have lost money. This is having its effect today on baby boomers approaching retirement. Some real life choices must now be made that were not on this generation's menu a few decades ago. Had the segment of baby boomers now approaching age sixty-five experienced even a 7% return during this decade, their nest egg would have doubled. Their 401(k) plans would now be capable of yielding the kind of harvest that baby boomers had imagined when they first established those accounts. But if you were age fifty-five in the year 2000, and you were planning on retiring at age sixty-five, not only did your 401(k) not double, it likely went down in value. If you happened to be a little heavy in NASDAQ stocks, your portfolio could have quite easily taken up to a 50% hit or more.

When I teach my retirement workshops I find that even math majors have a hard time coming up with the answer to this one right away: If I lose 50% in the market, how much does the market have to go back up before I get even? Most will answer, "Fifty percent." Some will look at me as if to say, "Duh…if you lose 50%, and the market goes up 50%, then you're even!" But think about it for a moment. You have four quarters. I take away half of them. You now have two quarters. I give you back half of what I took away. How many quarters do you have? That's right. You now have three quarters. So, in order to give you back *all* the quarters you had, I have to return 100% of what I took away. But that is not the whole equation. We are talking about working money here. As the market was losing ground, you had less and less money working for you. To get back to the position you were in *originally*, the market would have to have a gain of 100%.

For example: If you invested $100,000 into a mutual fund that experienced a 20% loss, you would lose $20,000. The account value on your next statement would be $80,000.

Question: For you to get your statement balance back to $100,000, will a 20% gain recoup your loss?

Let's crunch the numbers: $80,000 x 20% = $16,000 $80,000 (your beginning balance) + $16,000 = $96,000

Answer: No, a 20% loss followed by a 20% gain does not get your principal back. In fact, to regain your original principal balance, you will need to get a 25% return.

REQUIRED RETURN TO REGAIN YOUR PRINCIPAL

%LOST	GAIN NEEDED%
20%	25%
30%	42.86%
40%	66.67%
50%	100%
60%	150%

Do you see why it's a little tricky to figure? And if the market has to go back up 100% to recover from a loss such as that described above, that game's over, folks. There simply is no recovery that will accommodate so large a loss.

All is not lost, however, if (and this is a big "if") you can stay healthy enough long enough to put in the additional years it will take you to rebuild your portfolio. Working a little overtime never hurt anyone, did it? And it may be just what you need to do to patch the hole left by the lost decade. It may be that the solution is as simple as having a little part-time work during your retirement years. On hearing that, you may feel as did the tourist upon seeing graffiti on the Eiffel Tower, "Hey, this wasn't in the brochure!" But it's not the end of the world. Many of my retired clients tell me that they grew restless and bored shortly after they retired. Many of them say they got a part-time job just to stay actively engaged. But working also has the side effect of keeping their portfolios healthy as well, which, they tell me, makes them happier. This added activity after retirement also seems especially helpful to those who have lost a spouse.

Redefining Retirement

It may be that we need to pause for a moment to redefine this thing we call retirement. We actually have the Germans to thank for our current concept of retirement. The welfare-state social systems in Germany go back to the days of the industrial revolution when, in 1889, Reich Chancellor Otto von Bismarck devised the principles of the state social insurance scheme designed to provide for the elderly and the disabled and their survivors. The word "retirement" means to "shrink back from something for the sake of seclusion" or to "retreat." It is somewhat of a misnomer. After all, what is it that we are retiring from? Now, granted, if you don't particularly like your job, then the idea of being free from that obligation probably is attractive to you. But if you enjoy what you're doing, why not continue it, if you can?

Steve Jobs died on October 5, 2011, and I have learned more about the Apple cofounder since his death than I ever knew about him when he was living. Jobs died of pancreatic cancer at the young age of fifty-six. He made an unprecedented impact on the world through the devices he pioneered, such as the iPod, iPhone and the iPad tablet computer. In little more than a decade, he took Apple from near-bankruptcy to being the world's second most valuable company around $80+ billion in cash reserves.

Sadly, most of what Jobs had to say about health and wealth and the meaning of life has come to the surface posthumously. It was only after he began to face his serious illness that he began sharing with the world some of his deeper thoughts. I have come to have respect for the man, not just because of his marketing genius or technical acumen, but for his candor and his insight on life. Here is a sample:

> *Your time is limited, so don't waste it living someone else's life. Don't be trapped by dogma—which is living with the results of other people's thinking. Don't let the noise of others' opinions drown out your own inner voice. And most important, have the courage to follow your heart and intuition. They somehow already know what you truly want to become.*

Everything else is secondary. ~ Steve Jobs, 2005 Stanford University Commencement Address

Jobs' mantra, when it came to work, was: "*Love what you do; do what you love.*" He admitted toward the end of his life that he was lucky to find out so early what he loved doing. But it makes the point that if we love what we do, then why give it up just because of the lines on a calendar? An old saying, albeit a macabre one, is told that *true* retirement is "holding a lily in a pine box." Just a hundred years ago, few people ever retired. They didn't make it to retirement age. But as a society, we are living longer now. Medical science is advancing exponentially. It's entirely possible that, in the near future, human hearts will be grown from our stem cells.

Do we need to consider a radical paradigm shift in our thinking about these years of our lives? I think so. The expression "sunset years" is being replaced by "sunburst years" in the vocabularies of many boomers. It is a time of reinvention. If working at something we feel good about doing adds to the quality of life and allows us to give back to society, while at the same time providing us with the additional income we will need for our senior years, then we should embrace it, not shun the thought of it.

A final thought here to my fellow baby boomers regarding this transition into your retirement years. Think back to when you were the happiest and most fun filled. What were you doing at that time? I'm going to venture a guess that it had something to do with learning something new, or helping somebody in need, or mentoring somebody in some life skill/value that would help shape that person's life. My point here is to stay engaged—our country needs you now more than ever, our young people need your guidance and leadership. The concepts of personal responsibility, entrepreneurship, and capitalism are values that need to be passed to the next generation. Stay engaged and make the last third of your life the best third.

CHAPTER SEVENTEEN

Take Care of Your Health; You May Need It

*"A man's health can be judged by which he takes
two at a time: pills or stairs."*

—Joan Welsh

When I was in my late thirties, I was having terrible back pain, to the point where something as simple as going up stairs could aggravate it. When I could take it no longer, I consulted a spinal doctor who, after an MRI and some other tests, recommended dangerous surgery. The doctor did not actually use the word, "dangerous." That's my word. But to me, any cutting on my back, surgical or otherwise, is dangerous. This was not good. The surgery was set for late December, and I began picturing myself in traction, recovering from the operation, while everyone else enjoyed celebrating the holidays. It was then that I decided to get a second opinion.

The second opinion did not involve surgery, but it did require that I start exercising and modify my diet to drop thirty pounds. Looking back now, I realize that I was on what I call an *accelerated-aging plan.* I was helping the natural aging process along by making poor lifestyle choices when it came to activity and diet. So I began the process of reversing the accelerated-aging plan and what happened over the course of the next several weeks was truly miraculous. I lost the majority of the weight and the back pain completely disappeared. Now, fifteen years later, I have kept the weight off and am still exercising. I can honestly say that I am healthier today than I was in my late thirties.

The Health-Wealth Correlation

I am convinced that maintaining good health is similar to investing. It requires patience and dedication, and it has to be done in increments. I am reminded of an old expression my father used to use: "By the inch, it's a cinch. By the mile, it's a trial." The parallels are endless when it comes to acquiring and maintaining health and acquiring and maintaining wealth:

- It doesn't happen overnight
- It's never too late to start
- It has a compounding effect

It took months of good decisions and determination for me to lose the weight and get healthy. Building wealth is like that. Good decisions made daily to save and invest instead of splurge and spend, eventually lead to wealth. I believe that regardless of your age or the current status of your health, it is never too late to start making improvements. The compounding effects of such a course will be evident more quickly than you might think. What you do today, and in the years prior to retirement, will determine in large measure the vitality, or lack of it, you will experience in your golden years.

Health and Successful Retirement

What it boils down to is that, in retirement, wealth needs to be combined with health to achieve the ultimate success—or on a more basic level, your survival. It does little good to invest systematically in your 401(k) and not your health, even though many do just that. I consider my practice as a financial advisor to be much like that of the doctor who gave me my second opinion. His diagnosis of my situation and his recommendation for a cure were holistic in nature...that is, based on my life as a whole. I prefer to use that approach as well in my professional practice. While the sign on my office door may not indicate it, my mission, when it comes to helping retirees, is to enable them to take greater control of their lives in every respect possible. I believe that when we take better care of our physical selves, we enhance our financial picture as well. In some cases, this can be converted into real dollars, especially if the retiree intends to continue working into his or her retirement years. That is a situation that will call for good health.

Working requires energy. It seems we start out each day with a certain amount of energy, and some have the misfortune simply to run out of it after a while...sort of like the bunny in the battery commercial. The poor little guy just slows down and gradually stops, while the other bunny, the one who still has energy (because he chose the right batteries, of course) just keeps on banging his drum as if he could go on forever. If you are bunny number one, working additional years after retirement may not be a pleasant, or even a viable, option. Investing in exercise for just an hour or so each day, four or five times per week, can make a world of difference in your energy level. Regular exercise combined with a healthy diet will make whatever we do, whether it be work or golf, more enjoyable.

I am convinced that you can build up your health just as you can build up your wealth, and the challenge of maintaining both is the same. What's required in each case is simply paying attention and making good decisions. Having said that, I do realize that sometimes life happens, and there are some events we cannot control. The famous runner, Jim Fix, comes to mind. Ironically, Fix died in 1984 because his arteries were clogged with too much cholesterol. He introduced thousands to the pleasures and benefits of physical fitness through his best-selling book, *The Complete Book of Running*. When Fix took up running in the 1960s, he weighed 220 pounds. By the time his book was published, he had trimmed down to 159 pounds. Some things come at us out of nowhere, and there is little we can do. There's not much we can do about our DNA, either. You could be doing all the right things, all your life, and still suffer a heart attack or get cancer. But that shouldn't cause us to scrap our healthy lifestyle and exchange it for a day that starts at Dunkin' Donuts for breakfast, followed by lunch at McDonald's and ends with us dining on kielbasa and Coca-Cola while shopping at Costco. There is an exception to every rule, of course, but it is still a proven fact that a diet high in fat and sugar will shorten our lives by as much as ten years or more.

Knowing How Old You Really Are

Websites are available today that enable us to plug in a few pieces of information and see our real age versus our chronological age. Go to www.realage.com and take the test; you may be surprised to discover how old you *really* are. In my case, due to my accelerated-aging plan, I was five years older than my real age when I first took the test. Needless to say, I was not happy. This discovery was one of my main sources of motivation for getting back into shape. I kept seeing that number, five, and wanted to get my years back. The good news is that, in most cases, you can.

Just as real benefits can accrue by daily investment in our wealth, daily investment in our health can have real and lasting benefits. As important as what we put into our mouths can be what we put in our minds. Reading about good health and fitness leads to good health and fitness.

I have great admiration for Zig Ziglar. I think he is one of the best motivational speakers of all time. I admire him, not just for his books and talks, but for his ideals and life philosophy. One of my favorite quotes goes like this: "You are what you are and you are where you are because of what has gone into your mind. You change what you are and you change where you are by changing what goes into your mind." I enthusiastically concur.

In his book *See You at the Top*, Zig tells his story of a return to physical fitness at age forty-five. "I had tried all of the quick weight loss diets," writes Zig, "none of which had any permanent effect. A physician gave me what I believe is still good common sense when he said, "If you eat more calories than you burn, you will gain weight. If you burn more calories than you eat, you will lose weight."

When he began his exercise program, Zig was exhausted after running one block. But he says that on the second day, he ran one block and a mailbox. Then he ran one block and two mailboxes, and so forth until he built up his endurance. Before long, he was able to run five miles each day. Knowing that about Zig adds new meaning to one of my favorite Ziglar quotes: "You don't have to be great to start, but you have to start to be great."

The Spiritual and Social Side of Life

I have come to believe that our to-do list for building our health needs to look something like this:

- Eat healthy foods
- Drink in moderation
- Attend church
- Spend time with good friends and family.

In case you are wondering what the last two items have to do with better health, please take the real age test at www.realage.com and find out. According to the Cleveland Clinic, staying connected spiritually and socially can add years to your life. The clinic has provided data from years of research by Dr. Mehmet Oz and his partner, Dr. Michael Rozian, which proves that being socially involved will lower our stress levels; those who isolate themselves have higher stress levels. Data also supports the idea that individuals who profess a belief in God and an afterlife have less anxiety about death, and, therefore, less stress.

The real-age test supports the notion that virtually everything you do in life is either adding years to your life or subtracting them. Understanding that can be the catalyst to making the sort of behavioral changes that can ensure a happy "rest of your life." I urge you to put this book down and go take the real-age test right now. I will wait for you.

Coping with Stress

No book about survival aimed at this generation would be complete without addressing stress. It is one of the silent killers affecting the baby boom generation. Medical science has established that stress increases your level of cortisol, often called the "stress hormone" because it is secreted in higher levels during the body's fight-or-flight response to stress. Cortisol is necessary, but too much of it can lead to such ailments as heart disease and high blood pressure. Stress also increases the body's production of homocysteine, which, in turn, promotes weight gain and higher blood pressure, and tends to place people at higher risk for diabetes.

When I give talks on foundational financial planning, I am referring to laying a good investment foundation first. I make the point that, without a proper financial foundation, any plan we put in place will crumble and collapse. The same principle applies to health. Let's face it; none of this investing stuff matters much if you're at home, confined to a sickbed.

Along with stress is another health predator that can interfere with our ultimate success in retirement: depression. A person may be physically healthy yet suffer from depression over the loss of a spouse, for example. This will cause him or her to be miserable during what should be the most carefree time of life. One woman with whom I am acquainted had millions of dollars in the bank, but she was unhappy until the day she died because she could not stop grieving over the death of her husband. The grieving process is natural, and no one can tell another how to deal with it. But prolonged grief can be as debilitating as a physical illness. We watched her isolate herself from friends and slip into full-blown depression. Next, her physical health failed and she died at the relatively young age of seventy-six, still grieving after eight years. Those who knew her well attributed the physical decline to her untreated depression. If you find yourself in a similar situation, seek professional help immediately. It is never too late until it's too late.

CHAPTER EIGHTEEN

How to Pull Off the Aging Thing

"Aging seems to be the only available way to live a long life."
—Kitty O'Neill Collins

Stop me if you've heard this one:

A retired couple strolling the beach one day comes across a genie's lamp. The man rubs the lamp and, sure enough, there's a puff of smoke and out comes a genie. In gratitude for her release, the genie grants them a wish. The man takes an appraising look at his spouse and says, "I'd like my wife to be thirty years younger than me." With a wave of her hand, the genie makes him ninety-two years old.

The truth is, time may be a great healer and educator, but it is a lousy beautician. But, as one old timer put it, "Getting old is not nearly as bad as the alternative." So the best approach to aging successfully is not going to be found in fountain-of-youth creams, lotions, potions, and dyes. It is going to come from within us and our attitude toward it. All the wisdom I have collected on the subject leads me to the conclusion that, in the end, it is not what happens to us, but it's how we *take* what happens to us that makes the difference. There are measures we can take to make our sunset years the best of our lives.

Stay Active, Stay Involved

I have noticed that whenever the advertising people have a message they want to get across to older America, they use models who are trim and happy with bright smiles and hair with flecks of silver. That is Madison Avenue's way of telling us how seniors should look and act. There's nothing wrong with that; it's just not the real world, that's all. Even those models, when the lights go off and the cameras stop rolling, are just like the rest of us with the same challenges and concerns. What I take away from those advertisements, however, is the truth that smiling is good. Being happy is a good thing. Being with people you love and interacting with them is a good thing.

But sometimes our culture works at cross purposes to that for older persons. At a time when people need and appreciate the company of others, society has a tendency to isolate them. I know some people who were once active and vibrant, involved and vital, who became sedentary and withdrawn. Some of it may have been physical, but the decline I witnessed was because of a lack of social interaction. Leaving behind a lifelong career can cause a sense of loss. It is critical to fill that vacuum with a healthy interest in the new world now offered by retirement. It is important to find new interests and meet new friends and allow no place for psychological cobwebs.

One young-at-heart senior citizen I know makes it her goal to meet and get to know one new person a week. She gets their e-mail address and phone number and keeps them in her phone. She didn't know what the word "networking" meant, but she was doing it.

If you have stories, tell them. People love stories. It's how they get to know you, and it lubricates the gears of social interaction.

Pay Attention to Your Physical Health

The older I get, the more of life's journey shows, and the more effort I have to put into staying physically fit. For one thing, my body and my fat have gotten to be close friends and it takes more effort to keep them apart these days. There are only two ways I know to do it: exercise and diet.

Exercise needs to be something you like doing. If your knees are in good shape, running or walking is good. If they aren't, then bicycling or using the elliptical trainer works for many. For some reason, it's easier on the knees. If you have a gym nearby, join it. It's a great way to make new friends and keep physically fit at the same time.

Even a modest program of weight lifting can work wonders for our physical well-being. The key to all of this is to get into a routine and stay with it. One hour of exercise a day will increase the quality of life immeasurably as we grow older.

It is a simple fact that if we eat more calories than we burn we will gain weight. If we burn more calories than we eat, we will lose weight. Keep the scales near the shower. Measuring your weight is the first step to regulating it.

Some diets may work, but I prefer balanced meals of smaller portions of low-fat, low-cholesterol foods. Changing just one detrimental eating habit is effective for many people. One man I know got down to what he considers his normal weight by simply eliminating desserts.

Watch Your Psychological Health

As we age, psychological changes take place that we may not even be aware of. The function of the left (analytical) side of our brain tends to slow down, while the right side, which is responsible for sensing and processing experiences, is enhanced. Our emotional well-being can be adversely affected as well if we allow our state of mind to become negative or stagnant. So, whatever you do, keep a positive outlook. If you don't feel happy, do happy things. Smile, laugh, sing, whistle, do something nice for others. It won't be long before your feelings will catch up to your actions.

Some advocate keeping the left brain stimulated by doing crossword puzzles or learning new skills or new languages. If you like to write, keep a journal. Chronicle not only your day-to-day activities, but compile your experiences of the past. It helps you better appreciate your knowledge and experience.

Retirement is an excellent opportunity to keep that promise you made to yourself years ago that you would read more. Set a goal to read something out of the ordinary. It will stretch you mentally. I asked a doctor friend of mine once if it was really true that laughter is the best medicine. I must have caught him right after he had attended a seminar on the subject. He proceeded to give me a scientific answer that I still remember. He said that laughter lowers blood pressure, relieves stress, boosts the immune system, releases endorphins, and increases muscle function.

"It can't be a chuckle, though," he said, earnestly. "It has to be a good old belly laugh. The kind that makes you shake all over."

Heard any good jokes lately?

The Importance of Money

The late Helen Gurley Brown, author and editor of *Cosmopolitan* magazine, once said, "After you're older, two things are possibly more important than any others: health and money." That view of life is a little too secular for me. I would have at least included some mention of the spiritual side of life and included God in the top three. But I have to agree with her that money is important in our older years. This is mainly true because it helps us maintain our independence longer. No one wants to be a burden on those they love, and money facilitates our being able to captain our ship and set our own course as we sail through our sunset years.

I believe that maintaining the same standard of living during your retirement years as you did during your working years is a reasonable goal. While that may seem to be a tall order for some, it is achievable for most people if they are disciplined and determined.

The better stewards we are of our resources before we retire, the more use of them we will have when we are older. Simply put, that means live within your means and invest wisely. I recommend to any who are still in the workplace to take full advantage of any program offered by your employer, such as 401(k), 403(b), or 457 programs.

Living within your means is an elastic expression. Translated, it means that if you don't want your upkeep to be your downfall, then don't let your outflow exceed your income. Consumer debt is a prison. If you are in it, escape as soon as possible.

Those who have climbed Mount Everest say that the ascent is dangerous and treacherous, but the descent is even scarier. Experienced mountain climbers say that it is a matter of focus. While climbing the mountain, they always have the goal in view and they are striving to that point. During the descent, however, the discipline it took to climb upward has a tendency to fade, and it is easier to lose their footing.

In our retirement years, we have scaled the mountain, and we have survived the rigors of that upward climb. Now we must use the wisdom we have gained to continue making sure of our footholds.

Learning How To Measure Life

My wife, Michele, is one who knows the value of things and sometimes has to remind me. I am not just talking about material things, either. She specializes in helping me realize when I am immersed too deeply in my work, that it is necessary to stop and take a deep breath. Translated, that means that something as simple as taking in a walk and enjoying nature can put harmony back into a day that has become discordant and frustrating. Taking a little time to recharge the batteries is, after all, what makes the batteries work.

Our family is fond of refrigerator magnets. The metal skin of the refrigerator seems to be a natural gathering place for things that a magnetic business card can hold there, such as a scrawled phone number, maybe a stray recipe or two. It is a place where the snapshot of a friend can be seen hanging out with a dentist appointment or a to-do list. Occasionally, one of those little plastic-letter slogans will be deemed "refrigerator worthy" by someone in the Paul family. Recently, one caught my eye that read "Life is not measured by the number of breaths we take, but by the moments that take our breath away."

I agree.

CHAPTER NINETEEN

Getting it Together: Estate Planning Essentials

"Good fortune is what happens when opportunity meets with planning."
—Thomas Alva Edison

No guide to retirement survival would be complete without estate planning. It is important that you have at least the basic documents in place. At a minimum, these documents should be included in everyone's estate plans to protect them and make life easier for those coming after them:

- Power of Attorney—Written authorization that allows someone else to act on your behalf when you are unable to make your own financial decisions.
- Health Care Patient Advocate Directive—A document that specifies what actions should be taken for your health in the event you are no longer able to make to make your own decisions due to illness or incapacity.
- HIPPA Release—Written authorization that allows the disclosure of all your medical records to your health care agent.

- Nomination of Guardian-Conservator—A document that expresses your wishes on who takes care of you when you are not able to.
- 9.3 Deed—The re-titling of Real Estate Deeds to avoid probate and to maintain control with the title owners.

These really are just the most basic documents. Lack of proper estate planning can have far-reaching and unintended consequences. Most people do not know the detrimental effect that the failure to plan can have. If you leave your estate planning to the state you live in, it can have a very negative effect on your financial plan. Here are some common questions that are asked about estate planning:

I want to make sure that my children get everything. Is it okay to leave everything to my spouse?

This has the potential of creating an unintended disinheritance. This means that by doing this your children will get nothing. What happens if your spouse remarries and makes their assets joint with the new spouse and dies first? Everything will go to the new spouse and more than likely your children will get nothing. Or, if you leave everything to your spouse and they get sued, your spouse could lose everything and nothing would go to your children.

I want to avoid probate and own a house. Is it okay to put my children's names on my deed to my house?

This will avoid probate, but by doing that you may uncap your property taxes and your children will owe back taxes, penalties and interest. If you decide to sell that house and move, you have to get your children's permission to do that and they do not always give it. Lastly, by doing that you expose your house to pay their creditors so you may lose your house if they don't pay their bills or get sued. This means that your children will not only end up without the house, but you might also.

I want to avoid probate, is it a good idea to add one of my children to my bank account?

This will avoid probate, but if you want to leave your money to more than one person, the person named on the account has no legal obligation to share those assets with anyone else. Also again, you may lose those assets if your child is sued. There can be additional problems if this is done.

I have a special needs child, is it okay to leave my IRA to them?

If your child is on governmental assistance, this very well could disqualify them for the assistance. It is not permissible to leave them more money than what the limits are for the assistance. It is not good to leave the money to someone else to pay for the special needs child without a written document that specifies what to do with the money. Without a written document they have no have a legal obligation to support the special needs child with your money.

I live with my friend and want them to take what I have; do I need to do any special planning?

If you are not legally married to the person, then they may be excluded from any of your assets when you die. They also may be excluded from acting as your advocate if you become sick and cannot speak for yourself. This becomes more complicated if you have children. Your friend cannot legally make any decisions for you if you want or do not want to be kept alive. Your friend would have to go to the Probate Court and be appointed your Guardian to do that.

I have a General Durable Power of Attorney, is there anything that I should worry about?

A General Durable Power of Attorney is like giving someone a blank check and saying here go be me. With that General Durable Power of Attorney they can do anything you could do, like withdraw all the money out of your bank. Be very careful who you give that power to. What happens if the person you gave that power to becomes mentally incapacitated? They could sell your house, sign your name to obligations you know nothing about or take all your money. Be sure the person on the General Durable Power of Attorney is the one you want and trust.

I have a will. That means I do <u>not</u> have to go to Probate Court, right?

Wrong. If you have a will and have only your name on your accounts or house, then your heirs will have to go to Probate Court. The Judge then has to order the assets to go where you said for them to go in your will.

I have gotten divorced and left my ex-spouse on as the beneficiary of my insurance policy. Will my children get the money?

NO. When you get divorced, the papers are supposed to say that your ex spouse will not get anything with their name on it. However, this is not always the case. If you remarry and do not change the beneficiary, your ex spouse will get the money and not your current spouse.

My spouse is not a United States citizen, does that matter?

There are some tax disadvantages that a spouse that is not a United States citizen faces. Also, they may not be able to receive any money from you if it is more than what the amount is that will not be taxed by the federal estate tax. Special precautions may need to be taken to make sure your spouse gets the money, has access to the money without incurring unnecessary taxes.

When you have your financial plan reviewed by a competent financial planner they can help you avoid some of these problems or at least have you speak to a qualified estate planning attorney. If you have any questions, please ask a qualified estate planning attorney to help you clarify what you need to do. Do not trust what you may read on the internet, believe it or not, it is not always true. Boilerplate solutions may work in some situations, but in some instances you may find yourself woefully short of what you hoped to accomplish.

Is a Trust Right for You?

It is a good question to ask. A trust is not right for every situation. Some of these situations include, but may not be limited to:

- Property in another country e.g. Canada.
- A relatively small estate where there are no other issues.
- If it is known that the beneficiaries are going to contest everything the Trustee is going to do, court supervision and approval may be better.
- Everything will be passed by beneficiary designation and it does not matter what the beneficiary may do with the inheritance.

- Everyone is of the age of majority in their state.
- No beneficiary is going to be sued.
- No beneficiary is going to be divorced.
- No beneficiary is special needs or on governmental assistance.
- You do not mind if a stranger has the final determination of how your money will be split up.
- You do not mind if your state determines who gets your money and when.
- You do not mind if your state determines where you will live if you become disabled and what bills will be paid or gifts made.

As it can be seen, in most cases, a revocable living trust is a better plan for maintaining control over your affairs while you are alive or if you become disabled or when you die. A good revocable living trust should plan for the three seasons of your life: When you are alive and well, if you are disabled and after you die.

If you have children and they are minors, or not the best stewards of money, or would do something with the money you do not approve of, a trust is a must.

If you are married and want to ensure that your hard earned money gets to your children and does not go to pay your surviving spouses creditors if they get sued, or to their new family if they remarry, a trust is a must.

If your beneficiary is in a profession that is apt to be sued and you want your beneficiary to not lose the money in a lawsuit, a trust is a must.

In most cases a trust is a better way to maintain control of your affairs while you are alive and after you pass away, but not always.

When we are talking about survival, we are not talking just about survival through the retirement years, but of the survival of your legacy, not just for yourselves, but your extended family, your children and grandchildren. Having the right documents in place is of paramount importance so you can facilitate the transfer of your wealth in the most tax-efficient and tax-advantageous way possible to your children and grandchildren. This is certainly going to help promote their survival, particularly in a world where entitlement programs like Social Security look very questionable for future generations, as well as for the Baby Boom generation. Proactive estate planning documents can go a long way in promoting very successful lives for both your children and grandchildren.

Our intention is that if you're passing on a rather sizeable legacy onto your children and grandchildren is that it's done not only in the most efficient way possible, but that you've set it up in such a way as to incentivize their lives. Too much money received too early, depending on a person's age and maturity level, can actually work against them. That's why we like the concept of the family incentive trust. This can be set up if you're leaving money to a younger person to incentivize their lives to go out and achieve. The whole idea is to help your family, your children, and grandchildren build character by going out and doing the hard work like you did to build your legacy. Whether it's going to college and allowing them to get so much from the trust if they reach a certain grade level, or it's matching their W-2 or 1099 wages.

Your trust can be constructed in a number of different ways to provide an incentive to them to go out and produce. Based on that production, it will actually trigger disbursements from the trust commensurate with the level of achievement. So the trust becomes more than just a document, it can actually change lives. It can help them live a life they otherwise might not have been able to experience, or to achieve a level of education or success they may not have been able to reach without amassing a large amount of debt.

I want to thank Gregory Hamilton, Attorney at Law, for his legal counsel and contributions to our discussions regarding estate planning. We strongly encourage anyone that has an estate that they want to transfer efficiently, to consult with an attorney. Do not necessarily look for the most inexpensive advice, because it's too important to not get this right! Sit down with counsel that is an expert in estate planning. They can provide legal advice to ensure that your documents are going to achieve exactly what you hope them to achieve, avoiding probate and efficiently passing your assets on to avoid as much tax as possible, and ultimately to incentivize your children and grandchildren to have a happy, prosperous life.

CHAPTER TWENTY

Choosing the Right Financial Advisor for YOU

"Last week is the time you should have either bought or sold, depending on what you didn't do."

—Anonymous

In the preface of this book, I told you about a couple who came into my office one day seeking financial advice. Their world had just been upended by a sudden market downturn that had wiped out a sizable chunk of their retirement savings. I remember the deep concern on their faces as they explained what had happened. For their ages, they were too heavily weighted in growth stocks and had very little in the way of "green money" in their portfolio. It was a traumatic loss for them because they had saved for years, just to have enough to pay for two things: their children's education and their own retirement. They had met the first goal successfully. The second one now appeared to be in danger. They were overwhelmed and lost about what direction they should take.

Because I work with it every day, I sometimes forget how utterly confusing the world of finance must surely appear to some people. As I thought about this couple's situation, I reflected on the most "lost" I had ever been. My wife and I were in Phoenix, Arizona, on business for the weekend, when we decided to head up to Flagstaff to see some friends. Our goal was to arrive back in Phoenix before dark, but we figured we had time to take the back roads on the return trip and enjoy the incredible scenery along the way. When we signed the contract for the Hertz rental car, we briefly discussed the merits of paying extra for the navigation device, but we opted to save the money instead, reasoning that the roads were straight and we had maps. Big mistake! Coming back, somewhat exhausted from the day's events of hiking and sightseeing, we found ourselves on a mountain road just as dark began to descend. We had somehow missed a turn we should have made. Maybe it was my internal compass, if there is such a thing, but after driving thirty-five miles the wrong way, I decided (at Michele's urging, to be honest) to stop and ask for directions. I carefully wrote them down, turn for turn, and finally, although a bit frazzled and irritable from the experience, we made it back to our Phoenix hotel.

Selecting a Guide Intelligently

When it comes to financial planning, you may not recognize that you need a guide until you experience a wrong turn, like the one experienced by the aforementioned couple who sat in my office, asking for what amounted to directions on their financial journey. To avoid getting lost in the maze of financial planning and money management, the guide you choose must be able to give you clear and correct advice. But whom can we trust? Trust plays a significant role in making such a selection. That is why many gravitate to their friends or relatives for advice, which is what the couple in my office had done. Their friends and relatives surely meant well, but their advice was invalid and detrimental to their situation. One reason trust is such an issue these days, is because there are so many differing opinions held by those who claim to be experts.

When advisors are polarized in their opinions, insisting that there is one way and one way only to manage assets, there is usually a reason for it. If that reason has to do with fees and commissions, then shame on the advisor. It is like a doctor prescribing medicine for a kickback on the pills. I believe, however, that such things are rare. Does greed ever motivate those in the financial profession? Does the name Madoff ring a bell? More often than not, however, I find that polarized opinions spring from the training that has been received by those who proffer these opinions, not from greed. Just as the medical profession has its zealots, so does the financial profession. This explains why there can be opposing schools of thought when it comes to how to manage wealth.

A friend of mine and I were recently discussing our bouts with back pain. As you can tell, I am passionate about exercise and proper diet. In my enthusiasm for my point of view on this matter, however, I found myself giving what amounted to medical advice on what my friend should do about his back pain. I stopped myself immediately. It is his back. I am not a doctor.

I do not want the responsibility for any decisions that he may make regarding treatment that he may or may not seek because of something I said. The next week, when I inquired about his pain, he told me that it was all better.

"What happened?" I asked.

"I went to my family doctor, and she prescribed muscle relaxers," he said. "Then I asked my chiropractor and he told me to come in for an adjustment."

"So which one did you listen to?" I asked.

"Both of them," he said. "I took the pills and I got an adjustment. All I know is my back is better."

That makes a compelling point, doesn't it? Which school of thought was correct? Perhaps both of them were. Could it be that each of these conflicting lines of thinking has validity? Sure it could. Why did the two professionals view diagnosis and treatment from such different angles? They came to their conclusions based on their individual training and experience. There is no evidence to suggest that either doctor had an ulterior motive.

It is like that among financial advisors, too. Because of their training and experience, one group of advisors may recommend equities for every solution. Another group of advisors, because of their training and experience, may exclude any use of equities and only recommend insurance solutions, such as annuities and life insurance. Usually, when there are extreme poles, the reality often lies in the sizable middle ground between them.

Both in life and money matters, some opposing points of view are neither right nor wrong. They are either intrinsically dual or they depend on how we view things, and what our personal preferences happen to be. Consider the image shown here, known as the Rubin vase/profile illusion. Do you see a vase or two human profiles looking at each other eye to eye? It is an optical illusion, of course. It goes to show how our perception of something can limit our thinking. See the foreground and it's a vase. See the background and you see profiles.

Interestingly, we can will ourselves to see one or the other, but we cannot see both at the same time. But arguing for vase versus face certainly misses the point. It is both a vase and a face. As it is true of so many things, arbitrarily taking sides can obscure a grander unity.

Questions to Ask Advisors

To make an intelligent decision about which financial advisor you will use, here is a guide you may find useful. By process of elimination, you may be able to pare down the field.

Ask About Credentials

No true professional will mind your asking about his/her qualifications and certifications. Instead of being insulted, the professional financial advisor will be pleased to tell you of his or her training and the designations of expertise that have come with it. You may find it on the advisor's business card and on the office wall, as well. Comment on the designations. When you see letters after his or her name on the business card, ask what those mean. If they still look like alphabet soup to you, then ask again and again until you understand. Trust is a major factor in making a decision regarding how to handle money that you have worked your entire life to accumulate and now will depend on to see you through your retirement. I believe the following list contains the core designations in financial planning. You will see others, but if you fail to see at least one of the following designations, you may want to consider looking for another advisor. There is no substitute for the core training the following designations require:

- CFP® (Certified Financial Planner™)—CFPs have completed a two-year university-level financial planning course and passed a ten-hour exam covering nearly ninety topics, from group medical insurance to derivatives.
- CFA® (Chartered Financial Analyst®)—CFAs must pass three exams, each of which demands a minimum of 250 hours of study and includes corporate finance and financial statements.
- ChFC® (Chartered Financial Consultant)—The ChFC® designation was introduced in 1982 as an alternative to the CFP®. It has the same core curriculum as the CFP® plus a couple of additional courses but does not require a comprehensive board exam.
- PFS (Personal Financial Specialist)—PFSs are certified public accountants, who specialize in personal financial

planning. The credential requires a detailed exam and significant financial planning expertise.

- CIMA® (Certified Investment Management Analysts)—CIMAs focus on asset allocation and typically complete final coursework with the Haas School of Business at the University of California, Berkeley, or at the University of Pennsylvania's Wharton School of Business.
- RIA (Registered Investment Advisor)—Although not a designation, this is by far the highest level of commitment in serving the client's best interest. They are also subject to a state audit of the practice at any time. Because of the cost and additional oversight, most insurance and securities representatives are not set up as an RIA.

That is a partial list of certifications; there is no implied endorsement of one certification, or combination of certifications, over another. Some of them are duplicative, and some designations require more training than others. It lets you know, however, that certifications are important as a means by which to gauge not only knowledge but overall commitment to the profession.

Is education and certification always indicative of competence and trustworthiness? Perhaps not. I always give years of experience and good recommendations more points than letters after a name. But these are recognizable gauges that help you build the bond of trust you need to have with your financial advisor, and they let you know that you are dealing with someone who is responsible and accountable.

It's also important to note that to be in good standing as a Certified Financial Planner™, there is an ongoing requirement of thirty hours of continuing education that must be adhered to. Your credentials will be revoked for non-compliance. In addition, any violation of the code of ethics could be caused for suspension or revocation of the designation.

How Are You Compensated?

This is not a personal question; it is a business question. You are not asking the advisor how much money he or she makes per year, you simply want to know if there are possible conflicts of interest. Knowing how your advisor is compensated may help you evaluate the relative objectivity of the recommendations you receive. RIAs generally work on a fee-only or fee-plus-commission basis. Here are the basic types of compensation and what they mean to you:

- Fee only—Asset-based hourly or flat fees: Many RIAs charge a percentage of the assets they manage for you (typically 1–2%). This compensation method rewards your advisor for growing your portfolio. Hourly or flat fees are often associated with a specific, one-time service (e.g., developing a financial plan). The fee may vary by account size and service. In addition to these fees, you may pay commissions and/or other fees for execution of the trades your advisor makes and for custody of your assets.
- Fee plus commissions—Along with an advisory or financial planning fee, some advisors may receive a portion of

the commissions when you buy certain financial products that the advisor recommends, such as insurance policies or annuities.

- Commissions only—Advisors sometimes receive only compensation from sales commissions on the investments they buy and sell for you. This method may give the advisor an incentive to recommend that you buy and sell more often.
- Wrap fees—Sometimes advisors charge a "wrap fee," which is typically a single asset-based fee for both the advice they provide and the execution of the trades they make.

How Do You Approach Investing?

This is a trick question. A competent advisor probably will not answer it specifically until he or she knows more about what you wish to accomplish. So the right response here may be questions instead of statements: questions about you, your risk tolerance, your time horizon, your income needs, your tax situation, your other holdings, and many others. Just like a doctor would ask whether you are allergic to penicillin before prescribing it, the right advisor for you will get to know *you* before making any recommendations.

How Will We Work Together?

Good communication between you and your advisor is important. You will want to know who your contact person will be, and how often you will be talking to each other. In some cases, the firm's principal may conduct your initial meeting, and then turn your portfolio over to an associate or a team who actually manages it. If personal rapport is essential to you, ask to meet personally with your team.

Selecting the right advisor for you may require some legwork on your part, but the importance of the decision grows exponentially as the size of your holdings increases. Think of it as taking an expedition through unfamiliar territory, fraught with danger and adventure. You want someone who knows the land and can guide your steps expertly and safely, especially if you are retiring and are in the "red zone" of the financial playing field.

I Don't Want to Pay a Fee or Commission, I Can Do It Myself.

This is for the folks who have done their own investing or financial planning throughout their working years. Some of you may feel you have done a terrific job up to this point, and others may be wishing they had now met with an advisor. No matter what category you fall into, you need to seriously consider hiring a true retirement or income planning specialist for the following reasons:

- There can be no mistakes going forward. This is *the rest-of-your-life* money. If you are retired, mistakes can't be made up through additional contributions. The retirement assets you have amassed need to last for thirty or more years.
- Check your ego at the door. You don't know what you don't know. You don't have access to some of the best

planning strategies and investment vehicles available to retirees. Many of these savings and investment vehicles are only available through licensed advisors.

- Your spouse may have been the person you have relied on to handle all of the investment and financial planning responsibilities. Having a trusted advisor in place in the event of that person passing could be one of the most caring and helpful things you could do. You have a chance to help your spouse choose the right advisor. My advice is to make this critical decision as a team.

- What is more important than how your advisor is compensated is the value they bring to the table. The ability to produce a measurable difference in protecting and preserving your retirement is the key factor, not the fee he or she charges. If your annual return was 12% net of fees and the service was everything you expected and more, the fee charged would not be an issue. Is a "Wal-Mart" priced advisor really a true value if her or she offers lousy service and returns that don't keep up with any corresponding benchmark? My point is it's all relative. The performance and the service expectations need to be in balance. Simply put, are you getting fair value for the fee you're paying?

- It is not only about performance, it is just as much about protecting your portfolio. You need to be certain you are being properly rewarded for the level of risk you have assumed. In most cases we are able to reduce the amount of risk exposure by properly diversifying the portfolio.

Most have an overweighting in large cap growth stock, exposing the portfolio to additional risk. For example, in 2008 the S&P 500 was down 38%.

When it comes to managed money, for an RIA there are no commissions or surrender periods. Clients can leave at any time. This allows you to test drive any RIA firm knowing you can liquidate without penalty. This is why, when it comes to managed portfolios, I prefer fee-based as opposed to commission compensation. It's usually less overall cost to the client, and they are free to leave if they feel the advisor is not meeting their service or return expectations.

One final thought on this, as I am coming to a close in writing this book. Just this past week I had a problem with my right ear. It felt and sounded like I was underwater, which I ignored. Then it began to hurt, and that got my attention. For some reason when it comes to my health I have a bit of an "I can do it myself" attitude, so I understand this mindset that some investors have. I first tried—after going online of course—putting drops of hydrogen peroxide in my ear several times, which didn't work. Then I tried olive oil, which actually made my ear burn. Then a friend recommended I try clove oil, which also did not work. After all these failed attempts I headed to the drug store to purchase an earwax removal kit. After limited success of trying to shoot water in my ear after putting in their special solution, I finally decided to make an appointment with an ear specialist. The doctor quickly assessed the problem, took out an instrument and voila, instant relief, and I could hear again.

The moral of this story is, don't be afraid to talk to an expert who can provide help when you need it. Again, sometimes it is best to check your ego at the door and admit we can't be jacks-of-all-trades. When not having a qualified specialist can result in serious consequences to your health or financial well-being, it is crucial to seek professional advice.